John Bumstead

On the Wing

A Book For Sportsmen

John Bumstead

On the Wing

A Book For Sportsmen

ISBN/EAN: 9783742814005

Manufactured in Europe, USA, Canada, Australia, Japa

Cover: Foto ©Stingray / pixelio.de

Manufactured and distributed by brebook publishing software (www.brebook.com)

John Bumstead

On the Wing

ON THE WING.

A Book for Sportsmen.

BY JOHN BUMSTEAD.

WITH ILLUSTRATIONS.

BOSTON:
FIELDS, OSGOOD, & CO.,
SUCCESSORS TO TICKNOR AND FIELDS.
1869.

Entered according to Act of Congress, in the year 1869, by
FIELDS, OSGOOD, & CO.,
in the Clerk's Office of the District Court of the District of Massachusetts.

UNIVERSITY PRESS: WELCH, BIGELOW, & CO.,
CAMBRIDGE.

CONTENTS.

	PAGE
INTRODUCTORY	9
HOW TO SELECT A GUN	13
Three Classes of Guns	14
How to tell a good Gun	15
Prices of good Guns	18
What constitutes a suitable Gun	19
Shooting closely	20
The Barrels	21
The Stock	22
The Lock	23
How to get a good English Gun	23
Gunmakers	24
LOADING THE GUN	26
The proper Charge	28
Table of Proportions of Powder and Shot	30
Caution as to the Use of the Ramrod	32
Charger for weighing Powder and Shot	33
HOW TO CARRY THE GUN	35
Rules to be remembered	38
HOW TO SHOOT	40
HOW TO CLEAN THE GUN	50
To prevent Gun-barrels from Rusting	53
LONG *versus* SHORT GUNS	55
HEAVY AND LIGHT GUNS	59
TWO EYES *versus* ONE EYE	64
MUZZLE *versus* BREECH LOADERS	67

CONTENTS.

WOODCOCK-SHOOTING	78
When Woodcock come North	79
Where Woodcock make their Nests	80
Where to find Woodcock	81
How to flush Woodcock	82
Flight-Birds	84
Peculiar Trait of Woodcock	85
The Period of Moulting	89
How the Sharp Ring is produced	91
American and English Woodcock	92
Scandinavian Woodcock	92
The proper Charge for Woodcock	96
QUAIL-SHOOTING	97
Habits of the Quail	97
An Adventure with an old Quail	100
The Enemies of the Quail	101
How to hunt Quail	102
The Bishop of Quails	105
Quail withholding their Scent	106
Charge for Quail-Shooting	109
RUFFED GROUSE OR PARTRIDGE SHOOTING	110
The Flushing of the Partridge	110
Where Partridges are found	111
Pot-hunters	112
The Partridge in a Tree	113
The Nests of Partridges	114
Habits of Partridges	114
The Drumming of Partridges	115
European Partridges	116
Difficulty in shooting Partridges	117
The Food of Partridges	117
Names of Ruffed Grouse in different States	118
Proper Gun and Charge for Partridges	118
PINNATED GROUSE, OR PRAIRIE HEN	119
Manner of Hunting	119

CONTENTS.

WILSON'S SNIPE	121
When Snipe arrive in New England	121
How to shoot Snipe	122
How Snipe fly	123
The Peculiarities of Snipe	124
Snipe Shooting-Grounds	125
A Story of a Tame Snipe	126
Proper Gun and Charge for Snipe	128
BAY SHOOTING	129
Frank Forrester's Opinion of it	130
Black-Bellied Plover	131
Willett, or Stone Curlew	131
Red-Breasted Snipe	132
Clapper-Rail, or Mud-Hen	132
Esquimaux, or Short-Billed Curlew, &c.	133
WILD-FOWL SHOOTING	134
Wild-Duck Shooting	134
The best Season for shooting Ducks	134
Shooting on Lakes or Ponds	135
Varieties of Ducks on Northern and Western Lakes	137
Manner of shooting Ducks or Geese on Lakes or large Ponds	138
The Canvas-Back Duck	140
Toling Ducks	142
Boating Ducks	148
Netting Ducks	150
Dug-outs	152
Point Shooting	153
Harbor Shooting	154
Coot-Shooting	155
BRANT-SHOOTING	159
Manner of shooting Brant	160
RABBIT-SHOOTING	162
How to hunt Hares or Rabbits	164

CONTENTS.

RABBIT-SHOOTING — *Continued.*
    Tricks of Hares 165
    Where Hares can be found 166
    How Hares and Rabbits leap 167
    When to shoot at them 167
    Rabbits are not Hares, &c. 169

THE SETTER AND POINTER . . 171
    A new way of training them . . . 171
    What my Setter did, trained in this way . 176

SHOOTING-DRESS . . 178
    Game-Bags . . . 180
    Flasks and Pouches . . 182
    Gun-Wads and Caps . . 183
    Shot-Cartridges 184
    Recoil 186
    Scientific Matters 192

GUNPOWDER 199
    English and American Manufacturers . 200
    Different Qualities of Powder . . 200
    Coarse and Fine Powder . . . 201
    How Powder is made . . 202
    How to dry damp Powder . . 204

HOW GUN-BARRELS ARE MADE, &C. . . 205
    The Invention of the Gun, &c. 205
    Materials for Gun-barrels 208
    Counterfeit Barrels 211
    Laminated Steel 212
    Barrel Figure 214
    Wire-Twist and Damascus Iron 215
    Horse-Shoe Nails 221
    Stub-Iron and Steel 222
    Welding 226
    Boring and Grinding Gun-barrels . . 230
    The Patent Breech 232
    Laminated Steel Barrels . . . 234
    Steel Barrels 238

CONTENTS.

PIGEON-SHOOTING	240
CLOSING REMARKS	244
APPENDIX	251
Technical Names used by Gun-makers	251
Terms used by Sportsmen	255
Constitution and By-Laws of the Winthrop Shooting Club of Boston	256
Rules of Trap-Shooting adopted by the New York Sportsmen's Club	262
Game-Laws of Massachusetts	265
Game-Laws of New York	268
Summary of Game-Laws	274

ILLUSTRATIONS.

Canvas-Back Shooting	Frontispiece.
Dog, Guns, &c.	Page 13
Woodcock Boring	78
Woodcock-Shooting	88
A Bevy of Quail	97
The Partridge	110
Duck-Shooting on Ponds	135
Harbor Shooting	154
Brant	159
A Hare	162
A Setter	171
A Pointer	177
Wire-Twist and Damascus Barrel Iron	216
Barrel Iron twisted in Spirals	227
The Patent Breech	233

INTRODUCTORY.

IT is the author's intention in this book to give the novice in sportsmanship such suggestions and plans of operations as might naturally be demanded by him of an experienced sportsman; occasionally relating passages from his own experience, and throughout pursuing a course that shall enable the novice to apply any ideas of his own that he may have to the task of becoming a practical good shot. This book is intended more especially for the sportsman of New England. It applies particularly to brush-shooting, by which is meant all kinds of hunting and shooting of game-birds, in the fields and in the woods. But it will also apply generally to any part of the United States or Europe; for, in the writer's opinion, to be a good shot in New England is to be one the world over.

So much has been written for the benefit of the young sportsman, that it seems almost like a twice-told tale to proffer more advice upon the subject of sporting. But the ground has not yet been, nor is it soon likely to be, entirely covered. During the past century there has probably been no time when greater strides have been made in the improvement of the fowling-piece and musket than during the past five years. War has brought about a wonderful revolution in the construction of most of the engines of death. We have witnessed the introduction of iron-clad vessels, the Minie and Spencer rifles, and Colt's revolving pistol, and many corresponding improvements have been made in the fowling-piece.

The advantages of breech-loading guns are so apparent in the case of the musket, that probably no war will ever occur, either in Europe or America, without their general adoption. The breech-loading fowling-piece also is destined soon to be placed in the foremost rank of sporting-guns. How long it will retain that position can only be decided by time.

The sportsman's profession by no means enjoys the repute in this country that it does on the other side of the Atlantic. This state of things will doubtless eventually be changed for the better. Here, the occupation of the sportsman has been considered as too low for any person of mind and character to follow. There, it is held to impart a finish to education, of which no young man of ability and position would fail to avail himself.

This prejudice against the name of sportsman is partly due to the fact, that, owing to their entire absorption in business pursuits, Americans have no time left to indulge in a delightful recreation, — a recreation that, besides giving joy and pleasure, adds much to the health of whoever is sufficiently skilled to enjoy it. It is due also partly to the fact that in this country hunting has been chiefly confined to a class of men who have injured its reputation.

In imitation of our cousins across the water, we should strive to make ourselves a more active and healthy race, by field-exercises in hunting, ball-playing, and other athletic sports. These, if properly indulged in, will neutralize much of the evil that results from associations in the bar-room, and in many places of amusement, attended as they are with late hours and vicious habits. Any gentleman who can take his dog and gun, and go into the woods for a day or two, inhaling the fine bracing air of early morn, and knock over a brace of woodcock on the wing, stop the rabbit in his long leaps, or cut down the noble partridge in its flight, will make the sluggish blood dance in his veins, and add much to health and long life by this open, manly exercise.

Let not the ignorant in this matter think that the true sportsman follows his occupation for the sake of the game alone. Who would labor as the sportsman labors, merely to bag a few quail and woodcock, which he will perhaps give away on his return home? No, it is the *sport itself*— the excitement of the chase — which makes him so active and persevering. It must be experienced to be enjoyed, and must be loved to be experienced.

To the fields and woods then, with dog and gun, and enjoy this most manly of all exercises, which not only gives health and long life to the sportsman, but makes him a power to be felt in the nation's defence!

HOW TO SELECT A GUN.

IT is highly important for the young sportsman to understand the double-barrelled shot-gun sufficiently well to know what constitutes a serviceable article in the field, and to select judiciously a fowling-piece that shall prove convenient and pleasant in handling, and give success when used. The young student who wishes to follow the business of engineering and surveying must, before operating practically, study the use of the compass and the various instruments necessary in his profession. It is equally essential that the young sportsman be qualified to select his gun, and know how to use it, in order to become a practical good shot. Many interesting writers have neglected to treat this important subject, apparently taking it for granted that the novice can understand how to select his gun without consulting books or taking the advice of experienced friends. I propose to supply this serious omission; without, however, intending to give a learned dissertation upon the manufacture of guns, or a full description of the various parts and qualities that constitute a good gun. I shall treat of the subjects, "How to select," "How to load," "How to carry," and "How to shoot," each under its appropriate head; it being, in my opinion, impossible to deal satisfactorily with all these topics in one and the same discussion. In order to understand thoroughly the gun and its use, the sportsman must enter into the study of it with keen interest. He must not be contented with merely knowing how to load and shoot, without having attained any of that elegance and science in operating with his instrument which marks the artistic sportsman.

Fowling-pieces may be divided into three classes, with respect to size, weight, and calibre, according as they are intended for brush, or bay, or heavy duck shooting. And here I may observe that brush-shooting — as it is termed in this country, and particularly in the New England States — means all kinds of inland shooting in the fields and woods, and is the acknowledged standard for all kinds of sport with the gun. The description of the gun used for shooting woodcock, quail, and partridge will therefore answer for all the other sizes of guns hereafter named.

Sporting-guns, then, may be classified as follows:—

I. For brush-shooting the gun should weigh 7 lbs.; length of barrel, 28 to 30 inches; bore, 14 or 15.

II. For bay or pigeon shooting, or for ruffed grouse as

HOW TO SELECT A GUN.   15

a specialty, or for a light duck gun, the weight is 8 lbs.; length of barrel, 30 inches; bore, 11.

III. For a heavy duck gun, and for all kinds of wild-fowl shooting, the weight is 9½ lbs., length of barrel, 30 inches; bore, 11.

This comprises all the varieties of fowling-pieces ordinarily used for shooting the different species of game found in this country. And while there are so many opinions regarding the proper size, weight, length, and calibre of any gun that I cannot expect all sportsmen to agree with me in every particular, I believe, nevertheless, that most experienced shots will in the main coincide with the proportions above named.

A gun for brush-shooting that shall be easily and pleasantly handled, that will hold its shot well up to the mark, that shall have no waste iron or wood about it to fag the sportsman as he carries it in the hot months of summer and early autumn, ought to be of the following description: Length of barrel from nipple to muzzle, 28 to 30 inches; bore, 14 or 15. There is no objection to the calibre of 13, if the length of the barrel be proportionately increased. A well-made gun of these dimensions, if properly loaded and correctly held, will kill handsomely anything, from an old cock-partridge down to a snipe or salt-water peep.

In choosing a gun, be careful to notice the name of the manufacturer. If it be a high-priced English gun, and bear the name of Manton, Purdy, Greener, Westley Richards, or any other old established manufacturer, there is not much doubt about the quality of the material or the workmanship. Notice whether the barrels are made of laminated steel or stub-twist; the difference is discoverable in the figure. The former is variegated and beautifully blended, while the latter runs around the barrel in a simple plain spiral. One mark of a good gun, to be noticed in the selection, is that the riband of iron forming the barrel in a spiral form, and welded, can be seen where the welding-line meets. In good and high-priced guns they are $\frac{6}{16}$, and in the low-priced guns they are $\frac{5}{8}$ of an inch in width. In getting a gun made to order, have a narrow rib, as a wide one gives a clumsy and heavy appearance to the barrels. The ribs should be fastened to the barrels with soft-solder, and not brazed. The French and Germans braze their ribs, but the English hardly ever, as the heat necessary for brazing them injures the finished barrels.

The sight on the barrels should be small; it is not of much consequence any way, as we seldom use it. Some sportsmen have it taken off entirely, but it is better to let it remain on, as it adds to the finish of the gun; and there are times, in shooting late in the evening, or at early morning, when the sight will reflect and show itself to advantage. A small sight is the most desirable, and will give a more correct aim than a large one.

Examine the bore of the gun by calipers, which can be found at any gunsmith's shop. Compare the size of the bore at the breech end with the size at the muzzle, and examine two or three inches down the muzzle of the barrel, to see if at that distance it is of the same calibre as at the extreme muzzle end. This is of great importance, as no gun whatever can be expected to shoot well that is known to be what is termed "bell-muzzled." It is one of the tricks of the trade to make a barrel bell-muzzled, and the defect is not generally known. It should be sharply looked out for, especially in buying a high-priced gun. Barrel-makers, in finishing up their work, occasionally find the thickness of one barrel at the muzzle to be greater than that of the other; and this being a prominent point, easily detected by the purchaser, they sometimes remedy the error at the expense of the shooting power of the gun, by boring out the inside of one of the barrels, that the two may be left of even thickness at the muzzle. All experienced sportsmen know that this has a tendency to scatter the shot widely, and to make the shooting uncertain and defective.

No sportsman should think of purchasing a good English gun, without looking to find the *proof-marks* stamped upon the barrels near the breech, with the size of the bore struck in between. These proof-marks guarantee the safety of the gun, showing that it has been tried some four different times with more than double the quantity of powder and shot ordinarily used in a charge; and after such a trial it can be relied upon, as the "English laws are sure in their workings." The proof-houses are in London and Birmingham, and all English gun-barrels are proved in the same manner.

In selecting an English gun, do not be carried away with the idea of getting a superior article at about half-price, thinking that perhaps in this instance the

B

seller has made a mistake in the price. Even though the trader may say that they are extremely low, and that he is selling off the lot at reduced prices to close the invoice, he knows full well that his guns are an imposition, and will be proved so in the using. It is impossible to purchase a first-class English or French double-barrelled shot-gun at the low price of $30 or $40. I would advise the young sportsman to pay at least $75 for such a gun, and as much more as his pocket-book will allow, up to $125. He will thus obtain something near the worth of his money. It is wonderful how cleverly some of the barrel-makers in Birmingham and London imitate the high-priced guns with a cheap and spurious article. The "real twist," as the novice is wont to call it, is to be seen in the barrel, and the gun is finished throughout in a style well calculated to deceive the uninitiated. In these cheap guns the figure is beautifully brought out, and made to imitate the fine work of the laminated steel and Damascus barrels. This is effected entirely by a chemical process which eats into the barrels, leaving a fine figure. And this gun, finished so as to look almost as well as the more costly ones, is sold at a very reasonable price to close the invoice. Not only new, but even second-hand guns of the first quality, can rarely be obtained at very low prices; the material, the labor, and the manufacturer's name will seldom warrant a considerable reduction. And not unfrequently the second-hand guns made by Manton, Purdy, and other prominent English makers will bring at the present day their full value, and are sometimes sold at advanced prices.

In order further to observe what constitutes a suitable gun, put the barrels into the stock, throw the gun to the face, and see that the eye runs along the barrel to the sight in an easy and natural manner, with but a slight inclination of the head. If the bend of the stock suits the sportsman, his eye will meet the sight, as it were, at the breech end of the barrel, the aim being natural and correct. If the sight shows itself where it really is, at the muzzle, it indicates that the stock is too straight, and that the sportsman sees, not only the sight, but too much of the top of the barrel also. He must get his face lower down, and have a more crooked stock. If, on the contrary, the eye cannot find the sight unless the head is raised, it is evidence that the stock is too crooked for the form of the shooter. Long-necked and long-armed people, for the reasons here named, require a more crooked stock than those who have short necks and arms. The sportsman who wishes to be successful in shooting must select with especial care a gun that shall suit his strength, form, and style. If he desires to have a new gun made for him, he can almost always find at the gunmakers' or at the warehouses some gun that will meet his wants and come up to his face as desired ; and the angle for the new gun can easily be copied.

Have bar-locks in the gun of as good quality as can be afforded, and see that they pull off at about an even pressure. This is essential, for in shooting on the wing, if one trigger bears a pound more pressure than the other, its tendency is to throw the position of the gun out of the true line of aim, and consequently make poor shooting.

Avoid as much as possible all gaudiness in the look of the gun. Even if it be a really valuable one, the experienced sportsman will be inclined to doubt its merits. The Germans have flooded the American market with cheap guns, toggled off with German-silver trimmings, and highly-colored varnished stocks; which are by no means trustworthy, but are about as dangerous at one end as at the other.

Usually sportsmen of the United States think too much of shooting closely; that is, of having the charge of shot carried to a long distance, while covering a very small surface. Now, if our only *desideratum* were target-shooting, or the shooting of hens and turkeys, which used to take place at our old-fashioned Christmases and Thanksgivings, we admit that distance and closeness would be the standards. But if the gun is really to be used for brush-shooting, for killing woodcock, quail, and partridge, — which are certainly the most difficult game to kill clean and well, — a gun which concentrates its shot at a long distance would be a poor instrument to work with. Brush-shooting is generally made at short distances from the shooter, and resembles snap-shooting rather than open field-shooting. All practised sportsmen know that eight out of ten game-birds brought to bag are struck at from four to six rods' distance from the shooter. A gun of the kind just mentioned, if used in brush-shooting, would either tear the game, when held straight on to the bird, or in most cases would probably go clear of its mark altogether. A gun for brush-shooting, therefore, should throw its shot so that at a distance of 35 or 40 yards any bird coming within a circle of 30 square inches would not escape unhit by some one of the pellets.

In aiming at a bird on the wing, in the brush or open field, we do not exactly cover him, or bring the sight of the gun into an exact line with him (as we should do if using a rifle), but we are often an inch or two wide of the mark, and cannot have time to do better. In my own experience, when a bird at the distance above mentioned has come within a circle of about a barrel-head, and I have had no time for improvement, I have always considered the game secured.

A gun must therefore scatter fairly and evenly at the full average distance, in order to be serviceable in brush-shooting. Some guns, undoubtedly, scatter too widely, and these are not reliable. When I hear a sportsman say that he likes a gun that scatters well, I am apt to infer that he shoots indifferently, depending too much upon the spread of his shot. The best kind of gun for brush-shooting — which will not only shoot strongly, but will scatter its pellets evenly — is that above mentioned, with the 28-inch barrel, the gauge 14, and a weight of from $6\frac{3}{4}$ to 7.

I prefer laminated steel barrels (in which the iron and steel are mixed together before welding), but have used stub-twist iron barrels, which do their work equally well. The former are a little stronger and more elastic, and will endure rather more hard work; but either will probably last as long as the owner desires, and either will be safe and satisfactory.

When held to the shoulder, the gun should balance itself from the natural position in the left hand. The muzzle should incline to tip up, rather than down, for a gun that is muzzle-heavy soon becomes tiresome to lift. A thin muzzle is considered preferable to a thick one, as the hunter does not wish to carry about a superfluous weight of iron.

In selecting a gun, get a good fair breadth of barrels at the breech. Be particular to have the ramrod thimbles large. I never saw one too large, and in light guns few are large enough. Of all things the most desirable in using a gun is a large, substantial loading-rod, made from well-seasoned hickory, white oak, or beef-wood, — the latter is preferable, — with a large wormer attached. Let the rod be as long as possible without weakening the stock, so that by the wormer you can recover any substance in the chambers. I would recommend a small or medium-sized rib between the barrels, as a large rib makes the gun look heavy and out of proportion. Also the false breech of the gun should be made a little elevated, so that in forty-yards' shooting the shot will hold up well to the sight of the gun. If the breech be too low, in shooting at that distance at point-blank the centre of the charge of shot will fall from four to six inches below the mark.

I prefer an English black-walnut stock, as it is generally lighter than the American wood, and finer grain, although the latter lessens the recoil somewhat more. It should be finished in oil without varnish. If varnished, unless well rubbed down, a smart knock against it shows a spot, and the stock thus soon comes to look old; while the oil-finish, on the other hand, is rather improved by wear.

One extremely important point in a lock should be noticed. The hammer at half-cock should be at such a distance from the nipple that the cap can be put on, but not so distant that a slip from the thumb, either in bringing it to half-cock or in letting it down on the cap, will explode the cap and discharge the gun. If this rule were uniformly attended to, many fatal accidents would be prevented. We often hear of such accidents, arising from gross carelessness in allowing the dogs to spring upon the person while the gun is in hand. Not unfrequently the dogs, in slipping down, strike the hammers, and bring them almost to half-cock; then letting them spring back, they strike the caps with sufficient force to discharge the gun. Particularly see that, when the gun comes to the shoulder, the right forefinger easily reaches the forward trigger. If it does not, you will often be troubled, especially when you want to get in both barrels on the rise of more than one bird; and if you wear an overcoat, the difficulty will be increased, as the coat shortens the reach of the arm.

In order to obtain a good English fowling-piece at a fair price, I would advise going to some leading gunmaker in one of our principal cities, and obtaining by his means the barrels of the requisite proportions, made at some well-known English manufactory. Select also the locks, and, having the gun fitted to your shoulder, arms, strength, and style of using, get it stocked and finished up to suit your taste. Almost any of the prominent gunmakers in our Atlantic cities can satisfy you; their work and judgment can be depended upon, and in this way an English gun can be got up at much less cost than would be required for importing one. The high rates of duties and exchange make the English finished guns very expensive, especially while the premium on gold is so high as it is at present.

In Boston I would recommend Joseph Tonks as the gunmaker *par excellence* for judgment and workmanship. Schaefer and Werner also do good work, and manufacture high-priced guns. Mr. Tonks took the Gold Medal at the last Mechanics' Fair in Boston, and is also in the United States a leader in the manufacture of English breech-loading double-barrelled shot-guns. Both of these makers can show as good work as is to be found in any part of the country. In New York, Patrick Mullen, and in Philadelphia, Evans, are the leading gunmakers.

Origin of the English Proof-Marks.

The barrel-makers of England, having suffered long for the want of some test in the proving of their barrels, and feeling the importance of some protection to their trade, established a proof-house where the proving of gun-barrels by heavy charges of powder and ball could be made. This association was subsequently incorporated by an act of Parliament, in 1813. But the law being disregarded in the sale of large quantities of inferior and unsafe barrels, the government, in 1815, passed a more stringent law, making it a fine of twenty pounds sterling for any gunmaker to make or to receive, any gun-barrels not duly proved under the prescribed act. The same penalty was imposed upon a forger of the proof-marks of either the London or Birmingham proof-house.

LOADING THE GUN.

IN loading the double-barrelled shot-gun, let the barrels be held perpendicularly, and fronting the sportsman, so that the right-hand barrel will come to the right. There will thus be no mistake as to which barrel is loaded first. My rule is to begin with the right-hand barrel. If both are empty, put the powder first into the right barrel and then into the left, following each with a cut wad and the shot, then the caps alternately. This is far preferable to the practice of loading one barrel entirely before beginning with the other. The latter method is not so expeditious as the former, and the loader is more likely to get confused by handling the powder-flask and shot-pouch a second time. If you have but one barrel to load, and have forgotten which is empty, cast your eye down to the hammers. The hammer of the loaded barrel will be at half-cock, while that of the empty barrel lies down upon the nipple. Always half-cock the loaded barrel before reloading the empty one, in order to prevent accidents. As the gun faces you perpendicularly, hold it by the left hand between the two upper fingers and the thumb, taking hold just below the muzzle. To guard against accidents, be very careful to keep the wrist and arm clear of the muzzle. By practice this method will become so natural as always to be spon-

LOADING THE GUN. 27

taneously adopted whenever you have any work to do about the gun. In general, always keep your fingers, arms, face, and body as much as possible away from the muzzle.

After letting your powder into the charger, close the flask by a clear snap; and before pouring the powder into the barrels, see that the charger is full, allowing for the depression made by the ball of the finger. Pour it into the barrels with a side movement, keeping the hand as much as possible from the muzzle; if it has just been discharged, *there may be fire left in the barrels*, in which case you would run a risk of losing your right hand. But by following carefully the rules here laid down, such a loss might be compromised by that of the tip of one or two fingers. Now put in your wad, which should be one size larger than the bore of the gun. Should it go hard, enter it edgewise, and turn it when in the barrel. Draw the ramrod from the pipes and ram home; but not so hard as to consolidate the powder. This may happen if the gun is foul, and will prevent the powder from igniting quickly. I have often seen sportsmen ram for a long time, as though the powder would do wonders if only well pounded. Next enter your shot from the pouch, with another wad upon it. When convenient, let this wad be lighter than the other, and do not pound down the shot; both the heavy wad and the pounding add much to the recoil. Before the wad reaches the shot, as the gun stands perpendicularly, strike the barrel a slight tap, which will level the shot within, before the wad is driven down upon it. Now recover the gun to the arm, putting on the caps, pressing them home by the hammers; then bringing the latter to half-cock, and the gun will be properly loaded. Before replacing the ramrod, slip it into the other barrel with two or three slight taps, which will drive the wad in place if it be somewhat started by the discharge of the other barrel.

The Proper Charge.

As a general rule in loading, I would recommend *bulk for bulk;* that is, the charger for the powder, if correct, will be evenly filled with shot. If any difference be made, especially in the case of larger and heavier guns, it is better to reduce the quantity of shot, as there is far greater danger of having too much shot than of having too much powder. The proportion of powder to shot by weight should be as 14 to 100. The proper average charge for the gun used in brush-shooting is 2¾ drachms of powder to 1¼ ounces of shot; using in summer Nos. 9 and 10 shot, in autumn No. 8, and in late fall shooting for partridge, No. 7. Do not use in such a gun over 3½ drachms of powder. Doubtless the gun will bear more; but overloading is as bad for a gun as over-eating is for the stomach. It disarranges its action. The gun will not do its work so well, to say nothing of the injury done to the arm by the recoil. No. 4 shot is as large as can be advantageously used in the brush-shooting gun for birds; for foxes, Nos. 2 and 3 will do; and for rabbits, No. 4 or 5. Generally sportsmen use too large shot. For it may be said that the smaller the shot well entered into any bird, the quicker he dies. When the shot enters the bird, the skin closes over the cavity, the bleeding is stopped, and the blood stagnates immediately. But when wounded with large shot, if the bird bleeds well, he will often hide and recover; or if he eventually die, he will not come to bag. This is especially the case in duck-shooting. Most sportsmen, and particularly novices, are disposed to use too many shot. This tendency should be guarded against. In a 14 gauge gun, $1\frac{1}{2}$ or 2 ounces of shot can never be so efficient as $1\frac{1}{4}$ ounces, because the charge rides in so many layers as to affect materially the shooting. Any one may convince himself of this fact by putting the large charge into a glass tube or vial of the same gauge as his gun. Having given much attention to the proper proportions of powder and shot, I have come to the conclusion that most sportsmen load too heavily. If too much powder be used, the tendency is to scatter the shot; if too much shot, the force is weakened, and a heavy recoil is felt. It is the shot that makes the recoil. Five drachms of powder and one ounce of shot will make less recoil than $3\frac{1}{2}$ drachms of powder and $1\frac{1}{2}$ ounces of shot.

Here let me correct the erroneous notion, common to young sportsmen, that a double quantity of powder and shot will kill game at twice the ordinary distance; or that an extra quantity of loading will in some way or other increase *pro rata* the chances of success. This current fallacy is in its simplicity similar to that entertained by the old hunter in the age of flint-locks. Having had a good chance at a large flock of wild ducks, and being asked why he did not kill more, he replied : "Well, it's always so; when I get a good chance for a big shot, I always have a little bit of a flint in the old gun. If I had only had a big flint, I should have killed a pile of them!"

For powder, I use Hazard's Duck-Shooting, medium size, No. 3 for brush-shooting, and a coarser article for duck-shooting. Fine powder is somewhat quicker, but it makes more dirt, strains the gun, — making more recoil, — and it does not hold the shot up to the mark so well at long distances. One great principle in the loading of any gun is, that a due proportion be preserved between the grain of the powder and the length of the barrel. A person who uses fine powder should also use very short barrels, and *vice versa*. Fine powder in a long barrel spends its strength before reaching the muzzle, straining the gun and weakening the force of the shot. The nearer the muzzle the powder burns, the greater the force of the charge.

I subjoin a table showing the due proportions of powder and shot, according to the rules above given.

Proportions of Powder and Shot according to the Rule of Bulk for Bulk.

1 ounce shot calls for	$2\frac{3}{10}$ drachms of powder.
$1\frac{1}{4}$ " " " "	$2\frac{3}{4}$ " " "
$1\frac{1}{2}$ " " " "	$3\frac{3}{5}$ " " "
$1\frac{3}{4}$ " " " "	4 " " "
2 " " " "	$4\frac{3}{5}$ " " "
$2\frac{1}{4}$ " " " "	$5\frac{1}{8}$ " " "
$2\frac{1}{2}$ " " " "	$5\frac{7}{10}$ " " "
$2\frac{3}{4}$ " " " "	$6\frac{3}{10}$ " " "
3 " " " "	$6\frac{7}{8}$ " " "

LOADING THE GUN. 31

For duck-shooting, or the shooting of wild-fowl from a boat, add twenty per centum, or one fifth, to the quantity of powder in each charge as above specified, in order to allow for the additional recoil occasioned by the boat, which lessens the force of the charge.

The following list of the number of pellets in each ounce of shot from an English manufactory (Walker and Parker's) will serve as a general guide. As, in different manufactories, the shot differ widely in the number of pellets per ounce, we can only give a table that will approximate to the general average. Ordinarily, English shot have a few more pellets to the ounce than American.

No. 10 has 1,726 pellets per ounce.
" 9 " 984 " " "
" 8 " 600 " " "
" 7 " 341 " " "
" 6 " 280 " " "
" 5 " 218 " " "
" 4 " 177 " " "
" 3 " 135 " " "
" 2 " 112 " " "
" 1 " 82 " " "
B " 75 " " "
BB " 58 " " "
A " 50 " " "
AA " 40 " " "

Mould Shot.

LG has 5½ pellets to the ounce.
MG " 9 " " " "
SG " 11 " " " "
SSG " 15 " " " '
SSSG " 17 " " " "

A Table of Tatham and Brothers' American Shot, showing the number of Pellets per Ounce.

	TT.	pellets	to	the	ounce	26
	T	"	"	"	"	30
	BBB	"	"	"	"	38
	BB	"	"	"	"	50
	B	"	"	"	"	63
No.	1	"	"	"	"	78
"	2	"	"	"	"	85
"	3	"	"	"	"	113
"	4	"	"	"	"	144
"	5	"	"	"	"	196
"	6	"	"	"	"	254
"	7	"	"	"	"	339
"	8	"	"	"	"	430
"	9	"	"	"	"	550
"	10	"	"	"	"	675
"	11	"	"	"	"	744
"	12	"	"	"	"	936

Caution as to the Use of the Ramrod.

Do not, as many do, put the ramrod into the loaded barrel while you are charging the second barrel with shot. For, should a good shot chance to show itself, you would not ordinarily have time to withdraw it, or you might possibly forget yourself, and shoot it away. Indeed, shooting away the ramrod is not an unfrequent occurrence with new beginners. A relative of mine once shot his away, and was fortunate enough to kill a partridge with it. This kind of a charge, however, is quite objectionable as a substitute for shot; and I would hardly recommend its use.

A Charger for Weighing Powder and Shot.

I have had made for my own use a charger, that answers the purpose of testing the weight of powder and shot in any powder-flask or shot-pouch that may be used; and I find it a very valuable article. It is made as follows: Take, in the first place, a cylinder tube of brass about one fourth of an inch in thickness and five eighths of an inch calibre, and adjust thereto a flat piston-rod half an inch wide by one fourth of an inch in thickness, — one side being marked for powder, and showing plainly the number of drachms and decimal parts thereof; the other side being marked for shot, and showing a scale of ounces with their decimal parts also; — and attach to the upper end of the rod a dasher made so as to fit the tube perfectly. To the lower end of the rod affix a stopper long enough to be also used for a handle.

By taking hold of the handle of the stopper and drawing down the piston, a space will be left between the dasher and the upper end of the tube, into which can be put a quantity of powder and shot, and the exact weight of the same will be indicated on each flat side of the shaft.

This charger will readily denote how much shot and powder the sportsman is using in his flask or pouch more correctly than many of the flasks now in use. It can also be made to indicate the proportionate quantity of each. If, for instance, the quantity of shot, as shown by this charger, be found to weigh one and a quarter ounces, by turning over to the other side of the shaft, it will be found to denote full two and three quarters drachms of powder for its complement, which is correct according to previous rules laid down of *bulk for bulk*. The slight difference in the weight of all good powder is so small as not much to affect this result.

HOW TO CARRY THE GUN.

IT is very important for the young sportsman to know how to carry the double-barrelled shot-gun correctly, when in the field ; so that he may be always ready for the springing of a bird on the wing, or for the jump of a rabbit or hare from his nest. Many hunters who would otherwise be fair sportsmen are so careless in carrying their fowling-pieces that they are never ready, but stumble along over the shooting-ground, unable, for want of system, to bring their gun to the shoulder in time.

System is as necessary in the field as in the counting-room or manufactory. Without order and method no one can succeed in anything. Let the young sportsman, therefore, adhere to fixed rules in carrying and handling his gun, and he will ever be ready to shoot his game when a good chance opens ; nor will he run the risk of killing his friends who may accompany him in his excursions.

After seeing that your gun is on the half or full-cock (if expecting game, I carry mine at full-cock), carry it in such a position that, if it should accidentally discharge itself, your companion may not be hurt. Doubtless it is difficult always to do this. When carrying the gun a great distance, through a long and tedious day's tramp, every change in its position brings relief; and this is where the danger lies. First weariness, then carelessness; then, perhaps, some dreadful accident.

If you are hunting in company, carry the gun to the left shoulder, across the breast, at such an angle that, in case of accident, it shall discharge over your friend's head. In the woods and fields, and when walking on a trail, do not put your gun over your shoulder, bringing the muzzle on a line with the head of your companion. Certainly he cannot use it as a looking-glass; and he ought to be made nervous by seeing its two eyes glowing at him, knowing, as he does, what a demon lurks within, and what a simpleton has control of it. Neither carry the gun at trail arms, for thus you will be likely to shoot your friend in the rear. If expecting a bird to flush, carry the gun across the breast to the left, at an angle of about 60°. Thus you will always be ready for a snap shot, and will never bring about an accident by carelessness.

Even when shooting alone, there is a great advantage in carrying the gun pointed as much as possible toward the sky. If woodcock or other game spring suddenly in thick covert, the gun can be dropped to the shoulder quite as soon as it can be lifted; and in case of vines, briers, or other obstacles hindering your ready sight, it is in a position to break them down, instead of being entangled by them. For brush-shooting in the summer months, when the covert is thick, this rule is almost indispensable. I have often known sportsmen to lift their gun into a bush, and damage their shooting in such a way as to lose the bird.

HOW TO CARRY THE GUN.

While alone or in company the sportsman may safely carry the gun on his shoulder, dropping the breech near his body, and thus get relief, being ready at the same time for any kind of game.

Only on one occasion do I remember having been in extreme danger from my own gun; and this case, which came near closing my shooting experience, I will relate for the safety of others.

While hunting alone in midwinter for the American hare, one of which the hound had started on a hill opposite, I endeavored to meet him, knowing his crossing-place. Walking very fast, and at times running, with my heavily-loaded gun parallel to the ground and at full-cock, the guard caught in a small oak staddle, pulling the gun back an arm's length, and bringing the muzzle almost in a line with my body; and, before I was aware, off it went with a fearful report. A few inches more, at most, and I should never have shot rabbits again!

When shooting in thick covert with company, make it a rule for the one outside to keep a certain position, so that the one who goes in will know the other's whereabouts, and not be likely to shoot him. One of the quickest and best shots I ever knew once put out his brother's eyes, in partridge-shooting, owing solely to his brother having changed his position without giving notice.

Do not carry your gun loaded and cocked under your arm, pointing towards the ground. The gun carried in this manner is always moving up and down, and should it go off it might injure your friends' or damage your own feet.

One other matter should be treated under this head; namely, the letting down the hammers of a loaded gun from full to half cock. I once saw a gun discharged in this way, in such wise that under different circumstances it might have caused a serious accident. It occurred from pulling the wrong trigger in the act of letting down the hammer. The thumb was on the right-hand lock or hammer, and the forefinger pulled the left-hand trigger instead of the right. The most deplorable accidents may occur in this way, as the process of letting down the hammers is very frequent.

Finally, never, under any circumstances whatever, point a gun, *loaded or unloaded*, toward any human being. It is the very extremity of foolhardiness and audacity to do so, and should hardly be forgiven by the person at whom the gun is aimed. Whoever does so gives sure proof that he knows nothing about a gun, and should never be trusted with one. The act is too reprehensible to be overlooked, even in sport; and he who indulges in it should at once be stigmatized as an ignorant and unsafe person.

Rules to be Remembered.

1st. Never, under any circumstances whatever, point a gun in sport, loaded or unloaded, toward any person or valuable animal. It is dangerous, and shows great ignorance.

2d. In loading a discharged barrel, see that the loaded barrel is at half-cock before commencing to load the other, and hold the gun perpendicularly, and in front of, and half an arm's length from you.

3d. In letting down the hammers, see that the muzzle of the gun is pointed upward; should you pull the wrong trigger, and discharge the gun, no harm will be done.

4th. In getting into or out of a carriage of any kind, or in going into a dwelling-house with a loaded gun, see that the caps are removed. If the gun be a breech-loader, withdraw the cartridges.

5th. Never leave a gun loaded; it causes it to rust, and puts it in great danger of bursting at the next discharge.

6th. Do not load too heavily, particularly with shot; and never omit to squib off your gun with powder before loading the regular charge, at the commencement of a hunt.

HOW TO SHOOT.

VARIOUS opinions are held by practised sportsmen and writers on sportsmanship as regards the best method for the novice to adopt in learning how to shoot. I would advise him, if he be an entire stranger to the gun, to begin by studying the instrument itself. Let him get acquainted with all its parts before commencing to use it. Let him, as far as possible, take the gun to pieces, for which process we will give some directions.

To take out the barrels from the stock, first half-cock the gun, slide the bolt that fastens the barrel to the stock, and then, by a peculiar, careful motion, the barrels may be removed without injury. By the use of a *nipple-wrench*, which should always be kept on hand, take out the nipples, and examine the manner in which they enter the barrels. If convenient, take out the breech-pin, and examine this also. Notice the conical form of the chamber which holds the powder; and the place where the fulminating powder from the cap enters through the nipple, and meets and ignites the powder in the chamber. If it be an English gun, examine the proof-stamps on the back of the barrels, see where they were made, and get acquainted with the number of proof-marks; notice the different styles, whether Birmingham or London.

HOW TO SHOOT. 41

After scrutinizing the barrels sufficiently, and finding them all right, put the parts together again. Draw out the ramrod from the pipes, and, letting both ends into the barrel, ascertain the length of the chamber. Then replacing the rod, put the caps on the nipples, and see that they are neither too tight nor too loose. When about two thirds on, they should tighten well, though not quite enough to open a seam in them. This is essential, that the nipples may be kept dry, and the gun be sure to discharge. Do not *force* the barrels in replacing them, but let them, as it were, find their own place; for, if you force them, you will show a joint at the top, where it meets the false breech. Next ram into each chamber some oiled tow, and, bringing the gun each time to the shoulder, snap the caps, so as to become used to the force of the locks and their mode of working. Now load both barrels with a fair charge of powder only, and, taking aim at some object, fire away. This will give you confidence, and you will begin to feel acquainted with your friend after hearing his voice. In firing, throw the gun to the shoulder, letting the eyes run along the barrels, and bringing the sight as close as possible to the object; then pull the trigger with a cap on. Always remember to drive in an oiled wad before using the caps, as the fulminating powder corrodes the chambers of the gun. After drawing the wads, load with light powder, and fire as soon as the object comes within range of the barrels.

Next, load with a drachm or so of powder, putting into each barrel about an half-ounce of shot. Take for a mark a wide board with a centre-spot either black, white, or red, about the size of a dollar. As soon as your sight, or barrel-range, meets the mark, blaze away, without stopping to think or dwell upon the aim. Keep as cool as if there were no shot in the gun. Fire away in this manner, without studying your aim, always covering the mark as nearly as you can, and never taking down your gun before it is discharged. No good shot with a fowling-piece always expects to make an exact aim at his target. If the line of his barrels comes within an inch or two of the mark, he is sure to pull trigger instantly, and is sure to hit. Do not pull the trigger with a jerk, but rather with a lively pressure which will not make the line of the barrels deviate. After shooting in this way for a dozen or twenty times, you will be very likely to hit the mark every time. If after much trial you do not hit, *study yourself*, that you may see where the error is, and correct it. It is presumed that you have good judgment and reasoning powers; if you have not, do not try to become a sportsman.

During all these operations, preserve a perfectly easy and natural position; and, when you are about to shoot, do not spend time and thought in adjusting yourself. And it is best, while beginning to practise with the target, to shoot entirely alone. Friends and companions standing about are apt to be merely a hindrance.

Having now attained sufficient skill to hit the target easily and accurately, without dwelling upon the sight, you should abandon target-practice, and shoot at the living mark. Go into the woods alone, and make it a rule not to shoot at anything unless it is "*On the Wing.*" Having now got through with your playthings, you must begin to shift for yourself with a new kind of target, — one that is always in the air, and moving with very various degrees of velocity. Shoot at almost anything that happens to be flying within a reasonable distance, — robins, sparrows, blue-jays, &c., — remembering that these are often more difficult to hit than the regular game-birds, whose flight is more steady. To make a fair show of work, you should not be more than three or four rods distant. Their bodies are so very small, and their flight so irregular, that even a crack shot will perhaps miss as many as he kills. In this practice use No. 9 shot. After making two or three such visits to the woods, having acquired confidence in yourself, and feeling at home with the gun, you are ready to seek for the real game. After making one fair bag, you will bid adieu forever both to target and small birds; for the bagging of one good partridge, quail, or woodcock will so set you up, in your own estimation, that to return to your old practice would be like a wholesale merchant's going back to an applestand.

Now, to perfect yourself, take a stanch, well-trained setter or pointer, and go into the open fields, searching for quail along some hedge or stone-wall. When your dog makes a point, stand firm and order him forward; or walk boldly up until the bird rises, then throw your gun upon him just as with the small birds and target. When the range of the barrel is upon the bird, or very nearly so, press the trigger, and you will be pretty sure to bring him down. Keep cool, and do not get nervous; tell your dog to be steady, and you will thus steady yourself. In most cases, especially if it be a quail or partridge, the bird will fly directly from you. If he does so, send home the shot into his dark, handsome feathers, and you will laugh to see him tumble. Load where you stand, before going forward to recover; for another quail may start up within ten feet of you. Never withhold your shot because you have not got the exact sight on the bird. Remember the rule above laid down for target-practice: Get as good a *visual line* as possible upon the bird, and bang away; and do not withhold your shot because you think the bird is two or three rods beyond a fair distance; the shot will overtake him and break his wing, or bring him down, so that he can be recovered.

Always, when pursuing game, walk slowly, and keep cool in all your movements. The excitement of the sport will itself be sure to make you quick enough; do not try to be too quick. When the bird, springing from the ground, has come to his flying-level, and flown a yard or two, then, if the ground is open, is the time to take him. This is far surer than a quick snapshot, especially in woodcock-shooting; it is almost impossible to shoot a cock as he springs from the ground, and before he strikes off on his course. But, in close-covert shooting, you must snap the bird on the first foot after he reaches the top of his spring.

In the case of partridges, after they have sprung

from the ground, and attained their regular movement (which takes place in a very short time), shoot for their backs, and well up, for they usually rise higher and higher for the first few rods; otherwise, if the bird is near, the shot will be apt to go under him. When on the cross-fire for any game-bird, first put your gun on to the bird from behind, and then move it forward in the direction in which he is going, according to his distance from you and the speed of his flight. Making the usual advance on the game, — which, at the distance of from thirty-five to forty-five yards, varies from a foot to a foot and a half, pull your trigger while the gun is still moving, and the bird will be sure to drop. A cross-fire is almost sure to kill, as the shot enters the most vulnerable part of the bird, — under the wing, where the feathers are thin and the vital organs most exposed. Besides this, your chance is good for breaking his wing, or getting a few pellets into his neck and head; in either of which cases he will be easily brought to bag. When going from you, it takes a smart-shooting gun to kill a quail or partridge at eight rods' distance. However, always shoot when you have half a chance, and you will thus often make a shot that will do you more good than if you had killed half a dozen birds near the gun. Here is where new beginners, and some old sportsmen, frequently make a great mistake; unless they see a sure chance to kill, they down gun, and let the bird pass. This habit is enough to prevent almost any one from becoming a crack shot. It causes doubt and uncertainty, and prevents one from ever trying a bird unless he comes within five or six rods, and offers a chance for a fair, open shot. To shoot well on the wing is a *science*, and your object is not merely to see how many birds you can bag in a given number of successive shots. This rule might perhaps do on the open moors of Europe, where the shooting is open and fair, but it will not succeed in this country. The young sportsman ought never to rest content with this kind of shooting; nor will he, when once he has become a fair shot. He will delight in cutting down quickly and cleanly the woodcock, or other bird, which he sees fly but a yard or a foot before it disappears behind a maple-top or a cluster of alders, — planting his shot so that when it comes out to the next open space it is a dead bird. This is the perfection of shooting on the wing : to be ready for any emergency of distance, speed, or angle of flight; or when getting but the merest glimpse of the yellow tail of the woodcock, as he disappears almost instantly. And this is the kind of shot which old sportsmen like to make. Let it be understood, in this connection, that the sportsman cannot always cut down every bird by a snap-shot. He will often miss, as he will often kill, when there is apparently no chance of success. But what does the sportsman go into the woods for? Is it for the sake of carrying his gun, powder, and shot through a long, hot day? If he does not take his chances as they offer, especially when shooting woodcock in July or August, he will never make the bag that the sportsman does who improves his chances.

Many good sportsmen erroneously suppose that a

HOW TO SHOOT. 47

gun which is partially foul shoots closer and with more force than a clean one, and say they can never do so well immediately after the gun is cleaned as after it has been fired several times. I cannot possibly see how the force of shot or ball in its passage along the barrel can be increased by foulness. Certainly the substance that helps fill up the passage cannot in any conceivable way add to the force. Suppose a ditch to be cut down the side of a mountain, of even width, and quite smooth on its sides and bottom ; would the force of the current of water passing through be increased by having stones and rubbish thrown into it? or by having the sides overgrown with grass and weeds? The farmer would not think so ; and neither do I believe that dirt in a gun or rifle can add to its propellant force. If possibly the shot is kept together longer by the sediment, this can happen only at the expense of force and the increase of the recoil.

While standing in momentary expectation of a shot at a flushed bird, do not spread your legs apart to get a particular attitude, as some sportsmen do. It may look rather artistic while at the stand of a pigeon-shoot ; but even there it is neither natural nor productive of success. For should the bird be flushed, and fly rapidly to the right, the sportsman could not conveniently recover his limbs from their strained position in season to get a good sight upon him. The better plan is to stand naturally, with the left side a little in advance, so that you may easily cover a bird flying to the right ; and if the feet are near together, as they should be, the shooter, by making a pivot of them, can always be ready for a bird flying to the left. In this way I have shot woodcock and rabbits, when in the former position it would have been impossible to turn the body and get the gun upon them. There is a further reason why the feet should be near together and the body but little bent. This position throws the weight of the gun more upon the body, and not so much upon the muscles of the arms, which, in the case of a heavy gun, not only weakens the whole body, but is likely to interfere with success in shooting.

Before going into the fields, oil the barrels of the gun on the top, near its breech and about the nipples. This will prevent the fulminating powder of the caps from injuring the staining of the barrels, and will keep off the rust. It can easily be washed off the next time the gun is cleaned.

The young sportsman must recollect that the rules laid down for the shooting of one kind of game-bird will apply in some degree to all. It is for him to use his judgment in the application, and to modify the rules according to the nature of his game. The woodcock is one of the most difficult of all game-birds to kill cleanly and handsomely; and the rules given for shooting it can easily be applied to partridge, quail, rabbit, or any other kind of inland game. They will also apply to duck-shooting from the boat, although this is to some extent a specialty by itself. The novice must have got some experience before he can kill a single duck going down-wind at the rate of ninety miles an hour. But if he be a good inland shot, it will not take long to make him a crack shot in this, as well as in all other kinds of wild-fowl-shooting.

It is impossible to give rules on this subject that will meet all the demands of the beginner. But almost any person adhering to the foregoing suggestions, and using ordinary judgment, can soon learn to kill handsomely and cleanly any bird or fowl that comes within a fair distance, no matter what the velocity or angle of flight may be.

HOW TO CLEAN THE GUN.

HAVE a tea-kettle of hot water ready on the stove, a pail of cold water, a small pitcher with a nose, some soft-soap in a dish, and the necessary cleaning-rods and tow. Let your cleaning be done out of doors, or in the barn or shed. Fill each of your empty barrels nearly full of cold water, and, after shaking it well several times, pour the water out, and repeat the operation. This takes off the dirtiest part, saves labor with the swab, and expedites the cleaning. Now, putting into each barrel a teaspoonful of soft soap, fill them both about half full of water; and with a swab of tow or brush of bristles, made for the purpose (which can be got at the stores for 25 cents), swab them up and down briskly. The brush being larger than the calibre of the barrel, works freely on the sides of it, and soon fills it with soap-suds. Pour in more water, and work lively; then turn out your suds on to the ground, and rinse with cold water. Then, filling both barrels with clear cold water, apply a tight-fitting swab of tow, ready prepared. Work quickly, pour out and rinse again, fill up again, and take a clean swab. In order to make the swab as tight as possible, wet the tow before entering it into the barrel. Generally leave the nipples open, and, as the water works through, fill up again. If this time you find the tow dirty, try again with clean water and tow; but if the tow shows no dirt, then rinse out the barrels.

Bring out your teakettle of hot water, — the water should not boil, — and fill the barrels slowly, leaving the nipples open. Let them stand a little while, and then pour the water out. Your barrels are now washed clean inside. Next wash the outsides with the warm water; and, taking the barrels into the kitchen, leave them in a warm place to drain. If you have a furnace, set them over the register, muzzles down, and they will soon dry.

While the barrels are drying, prepare some clean tow swabs, with which swab each barrel as soon and as briskly as you can, changing the tow as often as needful; and when you cannot find any signs of dirt, and have carefully reached and cleaned the chambers, make another swab, as tight-fitting as possible, of old cotton cloth instead of tow, for the final cleaning. Work this up and down briskly, and it will warm and clean the barrels; and when the cotton rag comes out unsoiled, your barrels are clean. Now with your finger put three or four drops of pure clarified oil (neat's foot is good for the purpose) on the cloth swab in different places, and swab the barrels a few times up to the muzzles. Drive into each chamber a tight, dry tow wad, with a little oil upon it, and let it remain there. It will absorb any moisture that may come from the nipples. Take a fine soft brush, with long hair, and brush around the nipples on the outside, finishing with a little oil on the brush. With a good piece of old cotton cloth, oil the barrels outside, and the pipes both outside and inside. Then rub off the oil, brush out the hammers, oil the inside of the stock a little, and wipe dry. Enter the barrels into the stock ; clean and oil the ramrod, and put it in the pipes ; put a cut wad into the muzzle of each barrel, and an oiled rag over both nipples, and let your hammers down upon the rag. Now put on your gun-case, as your gun is at last cleaned and ready for use.

To clean a gun is undoubtedly a hard job, and unless you love the gun you will be apt to slight your work. You cannot clean it as it should be cleaned in much less than an hour. This work is one of the chief objections to a muzzle-loading gun, and is perhaps the main reason why many sportsmen give up their shooting.

Do not trust the cleaning of your gun to a servant, unless you have one who can be depended upon ; and even then, watch him. It is very easy to have the muzzle clean, while rust is at work inside. I would not recommend taking out the nipples while cleaning, except occasionally, and when the shooting season is over. Then I would have the breech-pins taken out and examined, the barrels wiped dry, oiled inside, replaced, and put away in a warm place.

If a hard day's shooting leaves you too tired to clean your gun, I would recommend swabbing each barrel with tow, with a fair quantity of oil upon it. This will keep the rust from working until you can clean the gun, which should be done as soon as possible. Fancy jointed cleaning-rods soon get out of order, and are

HOW TO CLEAN THE GUN. 53

not so substantial as a good large rod of oak or hickory, which any gunsmith will make for you. Experience will teach all other details about the cleaning of the gun that are not given here.

To prevent Gun-barrels from Rusting.

When you put away your gun for the winter, in order to keep the barrels from rusting, fill them with melted mutton-tallow that has been properly purified. Then put percussion-caps on the nipples, well filled with the same, and press them home by the hammers. Afterwards grease the outside of the gun, the barrels, locks, and stock, and set it away in a safe place, with the cloth cover over all, in a perpendicular position, so that, in case the tallow gets melted, it need not run out and stain the floor, and make your wife dislike a gun. If your barrels are treated in this way, no rust will injure them. When the gun is wanted in the spring, set it upright for a while in a warm room, put the breech of the barrel into a pail of hot water, and keep it there until the tallow runs : then pour out and clean. An easier way, though not quite so thorough, is to oil the barrels well inside with clean mutton-tallow, and heat them by holding them inverted over a hot stove, letting the hot air pass up through the nipples. When the barrels are well heated inside, put them into the stock, arranging the nipples as in the other method. Drive down into the chambers a well-oiled tow wad, followed within the distance of about a foot by a tight cut wad. Let there be another wad between this and the muzzle, and still another in the muzzle itself. On the outside of the barrels put mutton-tallow, as before described. Put on the cloth case, and set the gun safely away. Thus treated, it will keep well, if in a clean dry place, and away from the salt sea air.

There is still another plan for keeping the barrels from rusting within. Get some large wooden rods turned by a lathe to about two sizes smaller than the barrel. If the barrel gauge is 13, a rod of the gauge of 15 will answer. These rods can be got at a trifling expense at any wood-turning factory.

Cover the rod (leaving about six inches for a handle) with cotton-flannel which has a fleece or nap, so that it will fill the bore snugly. Then having first oiled the barrels, put in the covered rod. This covered rod, fitting snugly, will prevent more air from getting into the barrels, while its flannel fleece will absorb whatever moisture they may contain. This will be found a very convenient way of preventing rust, and it does not involve as much labor as either of the other means suggested.

LONG *versus* SHORT GUNS.

FOR many years conflicting opinions have been held respecting the comparative merits of long and short guns.

Our fathers and grandfathers were great sticklers for long guns. The older the times, the longer the gun, appears to have been the rule. And at the present day there are many sportsmen of excellent judgment, who would never have a new gun, the barrels of which were less than from thirty-four to thirty-six inches in length.

I will not attempt to state the exact length at which a barrel will make the closest shots; for other circumstances must be taken into account; such as the force of the shot, and the general convenience of the shooter. Even should a gun shoot a little closer for being thirty-six or forty inches long, this trifling advantage is more than overcome by its ungainly length. Besides this inconvenience, the force of the shot must always be weakened in travelling through such a long barrel, unless powder be used coarse enough to burn to the muzzle. And, should we use the coarse-grained powder necessary to get up this extra amount of combustion, the gun would probably not be quick enough for shooting on the wing, especially in snap-shooting. Moreover, the extra friction of the shot, and the atmospheric pressure, in the barrels of the long gun, are sufficient, I think, to neutralize the extra force imparted by excessive combustion.

Many experiments have been made, both in this country and in Europe, in order to determine which of the two, a long or a short gun was the more servicable.

About thirty years ago, very short barrels with large bores were all the rage on the other side of the water, and they performed excellently. But a great error was made in increasing the size of the bore with the decrease in the length of the barrel. Had the bore been proportionately decreased, these guns would not have been given up for others of different dimensions.

There was formerly a definite proportion between the gauge and the length of the barrel. The English adopted the rule of one forty-eighth of the length of the barrel for the size of the bore ; and some adhere to that rule now.

But, in spite of conflicting opinions, one thing is quite certain, — the short guns of proper calibre, such as are now used, perform much better than the guns of the "long-gun age."

In this connection I will add a few extracts from an "Essay on Shooting," published about eighty years ago, and giving the experience and the conclusions of an English writer on this subject.

He says : "We have at different times compared barrels of all the intermediate lengths between 28 and 40 inches, and of nearly the same calibre, i. e. from

22 to 26; and these trials were made, both by firing the pieces from the shoulder, and from a firm block at an equal distance, and with equal weight of the same powder, and of the same shot.

"To avoid all possibility of error, the quires of paper at which we fired were fixed against planks, instead of being placed against a wall. From these trials, frequently repeated, we found that the shot pierced an equal number of sheets, whether it was fired from a barrel 28, 30, 32, 34, 36, 38, or 40 inches in length. Nay, more; we have compared two barrels of the same calibre, but one of them 33 and the other 66 inches long, by repeatedly firing them in the same manner as the others, at different distances, from 45 to 100 paces; and the results have always been the same, i. e. the barrel of 33 inches drove its shot through as many sheets of paper as that of 66 did. The conclusion from all this is, that the difference of 'ten inches' in the length of the barrel, which seems to be more than is ever insisted upon among sportsmen, produces no sensible difference in the range of the piece; and therefore that every one may please himself in the length of his barrel, without either detriment or advantage to the range.

"To obtain from a piece of the ordinary length the same effects as from a duck-gun, nothing more, perhaps, is necessary, than to have the barrel sufficiently strong to admit of the charge being doubled or trebled, as required, and the whole piece heavy enough to render the recoil supportable. A double charge of powder will not throw the shot or ball twice the distance, nor a treble charge to three times the distance the single charge does.

"This arises from the great resistance given by the air to the motion of the ball or shot, and which is proved to be fourfold if the velocity be doubled, and ninefold when the velocity is trebled, by an increase of powder.

"So great is the change in opinion of late, with regard to the proper length for gun-barrels, that many gunsmiths will now tell us that short barrels carry *farther* than long ones ; and the reason they give for this is the greater friction of the shot or ball in passing through a long barrel, by which their velocity is retarded and their force diminished."

Many sportsmen use very short guns in covert-shooting, and indeed for all kinds of brush-shooting, thinking that they can sight their game much more quickly with them. I doubt somewhat the correctness of this theory. Allowing that the 24-inch barrel can be handled more quickly than the 30-inch, it is nevertheless well known that very short guns are more difficult to hold up to their true aim than those of medium length. Nor are the latter, on being discharged, so apt to get out of the true line of sight as are the very short guns. This may readily be observed if the length of the barrels is reduced to the usual pistol length. The pistol-barrel is much more quickly brought to the sight, but it is also much more difficult to keep in the true position when discharged.

HEAVY AND LIGHT GUNS.

THERE has always been, and probably for some time there will continue to be, a great diversity of opinion with reference to the performance of heavy guns compared with that of lighter fowling-pieces; and not until the science of gun-making and shooting is developed much further than at present can we hope to arrive at a final decision. But the art of gun-making, and the general theory of loading and shooting, are now making rapid strides toward the definite settlement of this question. Evidences will, I believe, soon be at hand, which will determine with accuracy and certainty just how large a duck or other shot gun should be, to give the most complete satisfaction in its performance, when discharged from the shoulder. Much might be written on this subject without entirely exhausting it.

It is the author's opinion, that small double-barrelled shot-guns *proportionately* excel the large and heavy ones, both in closeness of carrying and in the force of the shot. Much of the superiority claimed for the latter gun lies, I think, more in the manner of loading than in the gun itself.

Many good judges, I am aware, think that the small gun will always perform as well as one that is heavier; and facts are sometimes brought to my notice which almost convince me that the lighter gun may always be used with advantage for all kinds of shooting. Nevertheless, I believe on the whole, that, at long distances, a gun weighing from 8½ to 9½ lbs. will throw its shot with more evenness and force than a gun weighing from 6½ to 7 lbs.

Some help may be afforded by considering the rifle. Although the shot-gun cannot be compared in its uses and results with the rifle of larger or smaller calibre, still there is no reason why the comparison of rifles with rifles should not lead to some definite results. Now, in the larger rifle you burn more powder, and use a heavier ball than in the smaller one, and, according to the laws of force, this ball is carried to a greater distance than the lighter one used in the smaller rifle and propelled by a smaller charge of powder. For it is a law in mechanics, that, if the applied force be proportionately increased, the greater the weight of any projectile, the greater will be its speed and the distance which it can traverse. This law must of course apply to the shot-gun. In the large-bored shot-gun we use more powder and a greater weight of shot, while the friction against the sides of the barrel is relatively the same as in the small gun; the shot must therefore travel with greater velocity and to a greater distance. We must therefore decide in favor of the greater projectile force of the large gun, in conformity to general mechanical laws.

But, judging from my own observation and experience, I should say that, even in duck-shooting, there is not in the heavy gun this proportionate difference in its execution ; for it is much more difficult to secure good and true proportions in the larger than in the smaller double-barrelled shot-guns.

The admirers of the heavy gun frequently remark that it will carry more shot for the charge, in shooting into a flock of duck or other water-fowl, and that consequently the chances for securing a quantity of game are increased. I question the correctness of this statement as it is commonly made, for the difference between the charge of shot for a gun of 7 lbs. and one of 8 lbs. will probably be only a quarter of an ounce, or a half-ounce at most, if the gun is properly loaded. The former increase would amount only to 20 per cent, — not such a wonderful difference, after all. And I would ask, moreover, Is there not, in the larger gun, a greater proportionate waste of force by the side-shot, which does not retain its momentum? In shooting at long distances with any gun, it is well known that the central portion of the charge of shot travels the farthest. Any one can prove this by shooting on the water in a still day. It will also be noticed, that, in very heavy guns, the shot on the side of the charge not only does not keep up with that in the centre, but much of it is wasted at short distances from the gun. This is especially the case when the charge of shot is too large for the charge of powder. These facts show that the opinion above cited is not well-founded. But they do not conflict with the previous statement, that, if the powder be proportionately increased, the central portion of the larger charge from the heavier gun will reach and kill at greater distances than the charge from the smaller gun. If we were always to shoot at large flocks of fowl, and from short distances, — say twenty-five or thirty yards, — then, I admit, we should be pretty sure to kill relatively more game with the large than with the small gun. But in shooting ducks from the boat or stand, it will usually be found that those which are cleanly killed and easily recovered are killed by the central portion of the charge of shot. Even should the sportsman with his extra shot occasionally knock down a few more water-fowl, is he always sure to recover them? It may be concluded that, in shooting at distances of forty yards and upwards, it is the central part of the charge which actually brings the game to hand, and that the momentum of this central portion is increased somewhat more in the larger than in the smaller gun, though not in *pro rata* proportion to the differences in the weight of the guns, or the increased charge.

It must be borne in mind that the small guns are generally finished in better proportions than the heavier guns, and that the forging and the hammer-hardening process gives far more density to the grain of the iron when it is thin. This greater density increases the elasticity, and diminishes the inertness of the barrels, during the process of combustion. It has been fully proved, in various ways, that the elasticity of all well-formed barrels contributes to the force with which they will shoot; so there can be no doubt that to check the elastic force of the barrel must, to a certain extent, weaken its force in execution. Any one who is sceptical as to the truth of this statement can test it by

HEAVY AND LIGHT GUNS.

covering his barrels with pewter or lead, or partially with rings or otherwise, and then discharging them with the usual quantity of powder and shot. He will find the force of the shot decidedly weakened; and, if the experiment be repeated a number of times, the covering will become entirely loose.

Without wishing to bias the opinions of others, I would therefore conclude, that for duck-shooting from stands and boats, where convenience of handling and excellence of shooting are alike to be considered, I should not want a gun weighing more than 9½ lbs. If two guns are to be used, as is usually the case in wildfowl-shooting, I would recommend the following sizes:

Heavy duck-gun, weight 9½ lbs., gauge 11.
Light duck-gun, weight 8½ lbs., gauge 11.

These guns can be readily handled, and will give strength enough for all the shooting to be found at present. The lighter gun will also serve very well for partridge, pigeon, or other inland shooting.

It is always best, whenever possible in duck-shooting, to have the gauges of the two guns exactly alike. It saves extra flasks, pouches, and wads, and removes the chance of getting the larger charge of powder and shot, in the hurry of loading, into the smaller gun, or *vice versa*.

TWO EYES *versus* ONE EYE.

IT has generally been thought quite impossible to shoot well "on the wing" without closing one eye at the time of making the shot. How often have I observed the tyro, even in shooting at a target, trying hard to keep one eye shut, as if this were one of the chief *desiderata* in shooting. Frequently he is to be seen holding the left hand over his eye, in the attempt to do what nature tells him not to. This was the old style of taking aim. Formerly, almost every new beginner after setting up his target, rested his gun across a barrel or box, and, as a matter of necessity, shut one eye in aiming at the object.

I admit that in rifle-shooting the left eye ought to be closed, in order to draw a bead exactly on the object aimed at. Nor in close target-practice with the shot-gun can the spot be accurately defined unless one eye is closed. But in shooting on the wing this closing one eye is quite unnecessary, and is, in my opinion, attended with disadvantages. Almost all excellent snap shots keep both eyes open; and a man hunting in July, while watching for his bird after having shot at it, wants both eyes wide open to *mark down*, whether he kills or not.

Many persons cannot understand how an accurate aim can be taken with both eyes open; though they seem quite able to understand how it is done with one eye closed. But, it may be asked, if you were driving a nail into a valuable piece of furniture, which would be irreparably injured if the hammer were to miss its stroke, would you shut one eye or not? Does the wood-chopper, as he swings his axe to strike every time into the same place, shut his left eye for a true aim? does the barber who shaves you? or the Indian who shoots with bow and arrow? In drilling rocks, when one man holds the drill for another to strike a tremendous blow with his sledge-hammer, does the striker squint, and aim so as to be sure to hit the iron drill, instead of breaking the arm of the holder? I never saw one that did. Indeed, you may search through all the mechanical arts in which it is necessary to make a correct line of work with the eye for a guide, and you will find that it is successfully done with both eyes open. All such work can be done by the experienced workman, with two eyes as well as with one.

The sportsman who shoots with both eyes open covers more space around him than one who closes one eye; he marks down his game better, and has a clearer knowledge of its flight. And with practice it will come easy to him to avoid shutting his eye. A child, in first using the hammer, would probably not hit a nail one time in five; but he will learn to hit it correctly with both eyes open, as readily as with one shut. Two eyes are made for almost all the uses in life, and their united vision will not ordinarily deceive us.

The sportsman who adopts the one-eye system is very apt to make poking-shots. It encourages a disposition to dwell too long on the aim, and does away with that open, off-hand style of shooting, attended by ease and elegance in the movements, which is the result of keeping both eyes open.

I know splendid shots, however, who always close one eye in aiming. Perhaps they could also have learned to strike, saw, and do all manner of mechanical labor with one eye; but this would prove nothing against the two-eye system. The visual line which is made when both eyes are open is natural and correct enough for any shooting on the wing, or at a sitting object: although in the latter case a person may have time to close one eye, still he can do as well with both open. I say, therefore, in shooting on the wing, have both eyes open.

MUZZLE *versus* BREECH LOADERS.

THE comparative merits of the muzzle and breech-loading shot-guns forms a question of no small interest at the present time. On the one hand, many old, experienced sportsmen, accustomed to the muzzle-loader, and capable of using it with a proficiency that entitles sporting to be called a science, cannot overcome a certain conservative feeling respecting their weapon, which leads them to look upon all attempts to simplify, or improve even, their old and well-tried favorite — all attempts to make sporting more easy, or, as they would say, more jaunty, than they have been accustomed to find it — with feelings wellnigh to aversion. On the other hand, the increasing taste for sporting which is developing among the best classes of our countrymen, and which I hope will keep pace with their increasing taste and cultivation, together with the wide varieties of game with which America abounds, and the freedom with which it can be followed, are bringing into the profession many persons with no predilections in favor of any weapon; rather, persons who are desirous of seeing in use only such as will conduce most to the enjoyment of the sportsman. The former object to the breech-loader as they would object to almost any improvement in the gun; the latter favor the principles of the breech-loader as steps at least in the direction of simplifying the use of the fowling-piece, and consequently tending to make it a more serviceable weapon.

For all practical purposes the breech-loading rifles and muskets have superseded the old-fashioned muzzle-loader, so much so that the leading nations of the world are making the breech-loader wellnigh universal in their armies. And even for sporting, — for shooting of the closest kind, — the breech-loading rifle is now a general favorite with our best marksmen.

As might be expected, the successful application of the breech-loading principle to the rifle led to the application of the same principle to the shot-gun. The two weapons, however, having very different uses, and differing widely in their construction, made the application of this principle to the latter gun a matter of much greater difficulty than its application to the former; and I have heard many old sportsmen declare, that in their opinion no breech-loading shot-gun ever could be made that would prove serviceable, and at the same time be perfectly safe.

But notwithstanding all the objections that have been brought against them, breech-loading fowling-pieces have been and are manufactured in large numbers, both in Europe and in this country. Also they are manufactured in a style of mechanical excellence that equals, if it does not surpass, that bestowed upon the muzzle-loaders. Then, too, they are commended by some of our best sportsmen, and in such a way that I cannot, even if I would, avoid a discussion of their merits in a work like the present.

I beg to state that what I shall express in this chapter I shall not say for the purpose of biassing the opinion of any one respecting any style of weapon, or the gun of any manufacturer; rather, I wish simply to bring forward for discussion the question of muzzle *versus* breech loaders, and if, in this discussion my own preferences should appear, let it be understood that I hold my opinions subject to such modifications as time and experience may suggest.

Let us, then, candidly enter upon the consideration of the question.

The advantages and disadvantages of the muzzle-loader are well known. The principal advantages consist of comparative safety in the discharge; simplicity in loading, — that is, no elaborate or delicate machinery required for either preparing or inserting the ammunition; and good execution with the shot. On the other hand, the principal disadvantages of this gun are, the loose form of its ammunition, the liability to danger in loading and the time involved in this operation, together with the great trouble of keeping the gun clean.

As opposed to these advantages and disadvantages in a gun, the breech-loader presents the following as its points of superiority.

1st. *Safety of Loading.* — It is claimed that in this respect the breech-loader has a manifest superiority; as, by inserting the charge at the breech, all liability to danger from premature explosion is avoided. This is a point of considerable importance, as we frequently hear of accidents arising from persons loading muzzle-loaders under excitement and in great haste. A gun, therefore, that can be charged without any risk of danger of this sort has quite an important point in its favor.

2d. *Rapidity and Convenience of Loading.*— In shooting on the wing, or in shooting of any kind, the weapon that will give the sportsman the greatest number of shots at the game, provided the shots be desirable ones, is entitled to be considered the more serviceable weapon. And the principle of loading at the breech would seem to give in this respect a decided advantage over loading at the muzzle, for it places the receiving place of the charge open, and immediately to the hand. Beside, loading at the breech requires that the charge for the gun be fixed; that is, prepared beforehand in the shape of cartridges. Ammunition fixed in this way, all in one compact piece, becomes much more convenient for handling than when carried separately, as powder, shot, caps, wads, &c. Indeed, all must admit that for rapidity and convenience of loading the breech-loaders have a decided advantage over the muzzle-loaders.

Without attempting further to specify other points of comparison favorable to the breech-loaders, I think that in the important points just named, — safety, rapidity, and convenience of loading, — all must admit that the principle of breech-loading guns presents certain advantages over the muzzle-loaders; and if we can secure these points, together with simplicity of mechanism, reliability and portability of ammunition, equal execution with the shot, and absolute safety in the discharge, we shall have a gun corresponding nearly if not quite to the ideal gun of our wishes.

Do the breech-loaders of to-day answer these latter requirements? That is the question. The answer will appear in an examination of the best styles of these guns now in the market.

Large manufactories of breech-loaders are now established in England and in France; and in both countries these guns have been adopted with a readiness and an enthusiasm without parallel in the history of sporting. At first they were accepted on account of their convenience alone; as in all the early trials of their powers of execution they fell in their results lamentably behind the muzzle-loaders. In this respect, however, the English guns particularly were rapidly improved, until at the present time they fully equal the best execution of the old guns.

The French breech-loaders I am not particularly conversant with. But very few have found their way into the American market; while the breech-loaders of English manufacture, however, have been brought here in quite large numbers, and have become well known to all of our best sportsmen. The latter guns are exceedingly handsome guns; and every one is accompanied by a "fit-out," not unworthy to "set before a king." All of these guns, at least all I have seen in this market, are what I may call tipping breech-loaders, and are constructed in one general way. In loading, the muzzle-end of the barrel is depressed, and the breech-end elevated from its bed and away from its abutment in the stock, for the purpose of inserting the cartridges in their places. This done, and a slight pressure applied to the breech-end of the barrel, it assumes its natural position in the stock, and the gun is fully charged.

An experienced sportsman, looking at one of these guns for the first time, observing the beauty of its finish, the simplicity, the elegance, and the ease of its movements, would be delighted with it certainly, as a piece of mechanism, if nothing more. But, when he thinks of the purpose for which this beautiful instrument is to be used, and considers that into those two tipped-up barrels are to be inserted two cartridges, each of about a finger size, yet filled with material of such power as in its explosion to put to their utmost strength all these ingenious contrivances for making the loading easy and rapid, and be liable to prove destructive of life should this ingenious mechanism by any mischance give way, he would examine it with particular care to see if it be safe to trust himself behind it.

I think such a sportsman would very naturally inquire if such a gun was considered perfectly safe. To which inquiry a dapper salesman standing by his side would very likely reply, "Perfectly safe, sir; no gun more so. Why, you could fire a solid, tight-fitting ball out of these barrels without starting them a hair." Notwithstanding this very strong indorsement of the gun, the sportsman would still have his doubts about its safety; and I don't think he would give them up even on a still further examination. Indeed, I don't think any amount of assurance would convince him that the disconnecting of the barrels from their abutment; that the complete separation of the chambers from their bases, were not signs of weakness; while his knowledge of what constitutes fitness in any gun, whether muzzle or breech loader, would lead him to conclude that movable barrels would be very liable to get out of order in springing even but slightly at their joints.

I know it will be said, in answer to all this, that these guns have been in use for some time, and have not given in the slightest degree any indication of weakness at the breech. But I can say in reply, that while I am not aware of any instances of their bursting, I have seen some of these guns that have sprung at the joints, making quite a gap in the abutment. And why should they not? for not only in my opinion is the piece of iron welded on to the barrels underneath, partly for a pivot to assist in tipping, and partly for security to the stock, too small and weak for the purpose desired, but the piece of iron which holds the barrels to the abutment seems to me to bear altogether too much strain for its position. Beside, this latter piece of iron is subjected to the constant wear and tear of loading, and it seems to me only reasonable that it should work loose. I must confess, therefore, that I do not think these tipping barrels scientifically mounted. I believe that the strain of explosion in the barrels should be borne equally or proportionally by the surrounding or supporting parts, instead of falling wholly upon a point underneath the barrels.

I have also another objection to state against the

4

use of these English tipping guns, arising from the complicated and extensive machinery required for fixing the ammunition ; and then a grave defect in the cartridge when prepared. In no weapon is greater simplicity required than in the fowling-piece and all things pertaining thereto. But the contrivances for fixing the ammunition for these tipping guns seems to have been constructed with the idea of making the manufacture of cartridges a highly professional operation. Go to any of the dealers in these foreign breech-loaders, and see what an array of instruments they will place before you. Spread them out upon a table, and you will see a collection of implements that will nearly rival the table of a first-class dentist. Then, too, the cartridges themselves are objectionable; being, in the first place, quite expensive, the shell or case alone costing some two cents each ; and, in the second place, the cases being made of paper, they are liable to get damp, and after being discharged to adhere to the barrels of the gun, particularly when the barrels get a little foul and heated from repeated shooting. I have seen them adhere to the barrels so firmly as to require forcing out from the muzzle of the gun : indeed, I have seen them withstand even this process of expulsion, by the breech-end or brass chamber of the cartridge giving away, and leaving the paper portion still adhering to the barrels, to be removed by some extractor or as best it might.

It is said that these cartridge-cases can be used two, three, or four times ; but I have observed that sportsmen generally use them only once, as they do not load so well after being once fired. These English tipping guns, therefore, do not seem to me to answer as wholly satisfactory weapons, on account of their peculiar construction on the one hand, and their decidedly objectionable ammunition on the other.

Is there, then, no satisfactory breech-loading shotgun, and have we only an impracticable theory for such a weapon? Before deciding this question let us examine carefully an American gun, a breech-loader, manufactured by Messrs. Ethan Allen & Co., of Worcester, Massachusetts. A superficial examination shows us that this gun equals in its finish the English guns, and at the same time is made of as good materials. Having found fault with the tipping breechloaders, we look to see if there is any modification of the principle in this American gun. Certainly there is. The barrels of this gun do not tip at all. In fact, they do not move at all in loading, but are secured in their position in a way that does not admit of the slightest spring or straining by any conceivable use. Of course, it being a breech-loader, there must be means of opening or getting at the breech-ends or chambers of the barrels for purposes of charging. This is done by making what I may call false chambers in the barrels of about two and a half inches in length, with an opening on the top for the purpose of slipping the cartridges into their real places or chambers. When the cartridges are properly placed in the real chambers of the barrels, the false or open chambers are firmly closed by a piece of iron fitting perfectly to its place, and with its attachments filling the space of the false chambers with the strength of solid steel, and giving ample resistance to the cartridges during their explosion. The covering or lid to these false chambers is very securely attached to the barrels, on one side by means of a hinge, and on the other side by means of a spring. One end fits snugly against the bases of the cartridges, the other against an iron abutment on the stock, which latter is securely fastened to a prolongation of the barrels. Indeed, these false chambers are part and parcel of the barrels themselves; and when closed they form a solid abutment against the cartridges. The cartridges are fired by the hammers striking each a steel rod running through the contents of the false chambers, and impinging upon the caps of the cartridges, giving to the latter a "central fire."

It will be seen that by this arrangement a great point is secured, — the absolute fixity of the barrels in their position. They are never moved. Then, too, the labor of loading is a very simple matter; and the gun can be charged as quickly as any breech-loader. In fact, so far as simplicity of mechanism is concerned, this gun is not a whit behind any gun in the market; while as regards its safety I don't think it can be doubted in this respect.

Again, the cartridges used in this gun have none of the objections that can be urged against those used in the English guns. The cartridge-cases are made of steel, and can be used, I should say, about as long as the gun itself. Two dozen of these cases come with each gun; and, so far as expense is concerned, they make the cost of the cartridges much less than the paper cases. Then there is no liability in their use to their giving trouble by adhering to the barrels, as is the case with the paper cartridges; and should a sportsman go out for a few weeks' shooting, he would not be burdened by an immense number, as fifty cases would answer all purposes, whereas a tipping gun with its paper cartridge-cases would need an extra person to carry the latter along; and then, should these paper cartridges happen to get a little damp or wet, the sportsman's hunt would all be up. Beside, no elaborate machinery is required to load these cartridges. A simple little hand-rammer about six inches long is all that is necessary.

With reference to the shooting of these American guns, I can say, from my own experience with them, that in execution they equal the best guns in the market, whether muzzle or breech loaders.

My opinion, then, as between the muzzle and breech loading guns, is, that the latter is the more serviceable weapon, and that it is to be the gun of the future. 'I am of opinion also that, of the breech-loaders to be found in our market, those made by Messrs. Allen & Co. are preferable to those made abroad, both on account of their convenience and safety.

The pains taken by the manufacturers in the making of these guns is such that I can confidently commend them to all who may wish good weapons. Messrs. Allen & Co. have long been known as the manufacturers of one of the best breech-loading rifles of the day, and they are not, therefore, novices in the art of gun-making.

WOODCOCK-SHOOTING.

WOODCOCK-SHOOTING may truly be termed the *ne plus ultra* of all shooting on the wing. Perhaps no other sport is so much enjoyed by the sportsmen of the United States, and especially of New England. However we may be able to knock over the quail, one with each barrel, or to put a sudden stop to the noble partridge while under full headway, let it but be known in the midst of the hunt that a woodcock is started, and all other game is forgotten.

There seems to be a special charm about this bird, which enlivens the sportsman, and gives joy and elasticity to his feelings. The sharp, peculiar ring that comes from the cock when he springs from the ground, once heard, is never forgotten. I know of nothing that will so soon stir the old retired hunter as that pleasant sound; nothing that will so renew in him the days of his boyhood, and set him to looking after his old double-barrelled gun and shooting-traps.

> "That joyous sound I love to hear,
> Ringing merrily, loud and clear."

In the behavior of this attractive bird there is a remarkable inconsistency. At times he is a tame, stupid, lazy, fluttering bird, which you can apparently knock over with a bean-pole; anon, rapid in flight, and cunning in his movements, he will dodge and turn sharp corners, and come back to his starting-point, where the novice sportsman would never think of finding him, showing in all a sagacity which makes him a respected bird. In July he is easily killed, if struck with the finest shot, and his flight is generally short, with about all the angles treated of in geometry. But in the months of October and November a woodcock is quite another creature. Instead of the gaunt and slim, comparatively tame and inferior-looking bird which you find in July, he has now become a much heavier one, with full, beautiful, dark variegated plumage and with a splendid yellow belly, which almost always shows itself when he is killed. He moves on his pinions with a velocity not exceeded by that of any other bird, from the time he is flushed until he is cut down by the snap shot. He startles, exhilarates, and leaves you, and is out of sight, with his sharp sound ringing in your ears, before you can draw a bead on him, or even get your gun to your shoulder, unless you are an expert shot.

The woodcock is a migratory bird, coming to the North in the months of March and April, sometimes when the snow is still on the ground. At such times he is found living in the dense woods, in warm, secluded places, under thick pines, and near a spring or stream of water, where often it would seem impossible for him to exist. This bird is thus an early immigrant. I recollect seeing one killed once under peculiar circumstances. It was about the 25th of February, while I was hunting rabbits in the woods, the snow lying several inches thick on the ground. On my way home toward night I was discussing with a brother Nimrod the probabilities of woodcock coming North so early in the season. My companion remarked that he did not suppose there was one to be found within the range of a hundred miles from us, when suddenly up sprang a cock with his sharp ring, as much as to say: "Here you have one, any way!" We had our guns on our shoulders, and our hands well gloved, for it was quite cold. My companion was able to get his gun on the bird first, and he knocked him over. It was a large framed bird, but quite poor. We should not, under ordinary circumstances, have shot him; but coming upon him so unexpectedly, and at such an untimely season, we could not but think that he was in a measure sent for our especial benefit.

Woodcock make their nests in the woods, often in wet, boggy places, on the ground, exposed to the rains, which often destroy them. They have generally five young in their broods, and hatch them out by the middle of May. It is generally believed that, when their nests or eggs are destroyed by water or otherwise, they build and lay again later in the season; and the difference in the size of the birds in the month of July warrants such a belief. Their eggs are of a dull cream-color, with a few scattered spots. In the New England States, woodcock pair off or mate about the 5th of April, when they begin to build their nests. These are made entirely by the female birds, and consist of a few dry leaves scratched together in a rough, careless manner. Both male and female birds take a part in incubation, during which period they are quite tame.

It is but seldom that a woodcock's nest is found. I once found a young brood of these birds while trouting, about the 10th of May, in an early spring; and they were certainly a funny-looking set of peeps, with their long bills, which seemed to be the principal part of them. With the exception of their bills, they very much resembled young chickens.

These interesting birds generally hang around their brooding-places, if they are undisturbed, and the season is favorable for boring. In one respect they resemble some of the human species. They live entirely by *boring*, — not their friends and neighbors, however, but mother-earth, in which they find bugs, flies, and other insects, and, above all, the angle-worm, of which they eat enormous quantities. Woodcock are generally found in low ground, and in the swamps and woods, among thick alders and maples, near a spring or stream of water, where they are well covered from the sunlight.

When the hunter first enters the swamp to ascertain if there are any cocks there, he must look for their boring-marks, and the spots they make, the latter of which are as white as chalk. The boring-holes are usually in thick clusters, and the experienced eye will readily tell whether they were made the night previous, or are old borings. If the hunter find any borings, he may expect to discover game near by, if not in the swamp itself, then on the side of the hill, or under a copse of maples or other cover that is contiguous. Look carefully for the spots and borings, and do not give up too soon because you do not find them; they may be there nevertheless. Let your dog work first on the outer edge of the swamp, among the alders and bushes, carefully keeping yourself in readiness about ten or fifteen yards behind him; for this is one of the very best places to find the cock at any season of the year. Work the dog with a bell, — a small one purchased for the purpose, — as otherwise he may soon be out of sight and hearing, and may possibly be on the point. When the bell cannot be heard, work up toward the dog, for the cock is sure to be not far from his nose.

You will soon learn to understand the movements of the dog by the sound of the bell, and be able to tell, even when he is out of sight, whether he is *making game* or not, that is, whether or not he is on the track of the bird; for the setter or pointer works up the track of a bird just as a hound does that of a rabbit. If the bird moves along, and makes a fresh track (as he will be likely to do when the dog is not too near him), the track will give off a strong scent, which excites the dog, and makes the starting and stopping sound to the bell. The sportsman, when he hears this sound, knows that his game is near. As the dog nears the bird, he will, if well trained, work slowly, and creep up until within a few feet of him. The bird, when it finds itself pursued, stops and stands ready for a spring. The dog, knowing this, comes to the full point, standing stanch and still, enjoying the beautiful sensation awakened by the smell of the bird itself. Both stand perfectly still, watching for, but unseen by, the other. The dog now trembles with excitement and pleasure, his tail sloping out behind and the saliva running from his mouth, and making a picture such as but few artists are capable of representing. The sportsman, when he sees the dog on the point, will either order him forward in order to flush the bird, or walk quietly but firmly up in front of, or on the side of the dog, put up the bird himself, and shoot him on the wing; while the dog remains stationary by his side, until odered to bring the game to hand.

I do not agree with those hunters who work the dog in the latter way. I have never walked up a game-bird with any dog that I have trained, and I would never train a dog for such flushing. I should rather choose my position in the woods, signalling the dog by the word "go" to put up the bird, and thus give me all the chances afforded by the open spaces in the thick brush and trees. I do not well see how a sportsman who goes alone into the woods in July or August can fill his bag, unless he manages in this way; for during these months the woodcock lie amid brush and underwood so dense that the shooter cannot at best see his bird at more than a few yards' distance when it is flushed; and, even should he be able to get his gun upon, it, he would be almost sure to tear the bird to pieces.

Some sportsmen, I am aware, claim that, under such

circumstances, the bird is apt to be chased by the dog. It may be so if the dog is not properly trained; but this can and should be remedied. The dog should be taught to drop or stand still when a cock or other bird is flushed. The pointer or setter may doubtless sometimes be tempted to chase the bird a few paces after he is flushed; but this tendency can be overcome with care. The method here described is certainly far the most desirable way to work a dog in any kind of brush-shooting. I never owned a dog, or saw one, that had been trained to put up his own birds after making the point, but what would set as regularly, and continue on the point as long, as dogs otherwise trained. A setter dog which I had trained to stand in this way, while pointing at once over a couple of woodcock, gave a party of four of us plenty of time to get our positions. Occasionally calling out to him the word "steady," he waited patiently on the point until we had secured good, open places; and then, at the word, he put up both birds, which one of the party dropped, taking a bird with each barrel.

The *flight-birds*, so called, while on their migratory passage to a warmer climate, are always fat, fine-looking birds, with full plumage. At this time — October and November — they fly very strongly, and usually at long distances, especially if started the second or third time. It is better, at this season of the year, to use No. 8 shot for woodcock.

In these months, the young sportsman who has heretofore thought it an easy matter to knock over a woodcock will be very apt to change his opinion; and

I think a little experience in hunting him at this season will very soon induce such a sportsman to consider him a wonderfully sagacious bird, rapid in flight, and hard to kill.

One rather peculiar trait about these birds, — and the same thing is to some extent true of other species, — is: that, late in the fall, at almost every flight, they will go toward the south, and you cannot get them back to the north again by any management. When once started, away they will go to the southward, over ploughed land and meadows, even though, at the second flushing you may have gone around in front of them to try and turn them back to a good cover in the alders, where there is fine feeding-ground. At such times it would seem as if they were drawn toward the south by some special attraction.

The general rules for shooting the woodcock will be found laid down in the section "How to Shoot"; but experience is the best teacher after all, especially when guided by a general knowledge of their habits of living and manner of flying. Woodcock is a species of game that good sportsmen delight to follow, and the pleasure derived from bringing them to bag is keenly held in remembrance when other sports are forgotten.

About the first or middle of August, when woodcock cannot be found in the woods and swamps, it is well to look for them in the contiguous cornfields. The corn at this time is sufficiently well grown to shade the ground, especially where the ground is low and damp. In these places the corn is usually quite thick, affording a good cover and fine feeding. I have known a dozen cocks to be found in one such patch of corn. If you happen to know that woodcock are in the corn, you can often do quite as well without the dog; and you will here find that good snap-shooting tells wonderfully! For the birds in their flight just top the tips of the corn, sail along a few feet, just showing their narrow wings, and in a moment are gone, — find out where, if you can. If you don't kill them at their first flight, and they go outside the corn-piece, they will probably turn to the right or left at the end of the piece, and enter the edge of the corn again; or perhaps lie in the grass which makes the headland, but a few feet distant from the end of the corn-rows. It is their nature, when flushed from such ground, to give a flourish and a sudden turn when coming to the end of the corn; and they will certainly put the sportsman off the track, if he be not well posted in their habits.

Hunt them thoroughly. They will often let the sportsman pass within a very few feet of them, without flushing. Much depends upon a knowledge of their movements, and in the marking of them down well in their flight. The sportsman who excels in marking down his game will get many more cock than the one who has no such tact; for there is much skill and judgment to be used in this particular, not only with woodcock, but with all kinds of game-birds. After having shot at your bird, cast your eye in the direction it went, and watch the next open space. If the bird does not pass, you have good reason to think that you have dropped it.

WOODCOCK-SHOOTING. 87

In the months of October and November, hunt your shooting-ground for woodcock often, if it be a good one. Even the next day after you have cleaned the game all out, you will probably make a fair bag. For at this season these *flight-birds* are driven rapidly to the southward by the frost; and if the sportsman be on the *qui vive*, he will be well paid for his trouble. When the weather grows warm after several frosty nights, they will often linger a few days, until another frost starts them along toward their sunny home.

The young sportsman must not expect to find woodcock in flocks or in bevies, like quail. He will seldom start more than one at a time, although there may be many near him. They are quite unsocial birds; and in their flight each one usually goes his own way, and looks out for himself.

The woodcock never alights upon trees, whatever to the contrary we may hear from farmers' boys, who talk of seeing him perched on dead trees in the woods. They mistake the woodpecker for him. Neither does he roost on bushes or fences, like many other birds. He has nothing to do with the vegetable kingdom, save to use it for a cover, and to make his frail nest with. He sticks to mother earth; and as she owes him a living, he presents his bill to her very often. His drafts are honored with the sweet nutriment of worms and flies. He paddles along in the dark night, and sometimes in the day, looking and smelling earnestly for his food. He has great powers of discovering where it lies; and his long, delicate bill will readily indicate when it strikes upon an angle-worm.

Then he has such a wonderful knack of drawing it out of the ground easily, quickly, and without apparent motion, that the sportsman, should he be fortunate enough to spy the operations of one of these birds, unless he watches closely will never suspect that the fellow is taking his dinner.

This remarkable bird has, for his principal protection, very keen sight; and his eyes, being set almost on the top of his head, and standing out large and full, give him a very extended range of vision, without which he would be liable to be pounced upon in the covert by foxes, minks, and other animals. His still movements also serve as a protection, as well as his color, the latter resembling that of the ground or the bark of the surrounding trees.

As previously stated, there is something that attaches the experienced sportsman to this bird more strongly than to any other, we might almost say, than to all others combined. One reason is, that the woodcock cannot be fully understood, no matter how closely he may be studied, for at every season he develops new traits of sagacity. Whether we call the woodcock, as many do, at all seasons of the year a foolish, simple bird, whose very simplicity accounts for the difficulty of finding him, or whether we give him the appellation of a very cunning bird, the experienced hunter well knows that, from one or both causes, it is more difficult to judge correctly of his movements than of any other game-bird that flies. Quail, partridges, and other birds have a law unto themselves, and are true to it, so that they can be calculated upon with tolera-

WOODCOCK SHOOTING.

ble certainty; but who can fully describe the woodcock in his flight, or predict with any confidence his whereabouts? In many respects he is the very opposite of the other game-birds found in the fields and woods; he is truly a night-bird.

In August, when cocks cannot be found in the swamps of alders or among the maples, look for them in the high and rolling grounds, particularly among the scrub-oaks and whortleberry bushes. You will sometimes find a few birds, but as they are at this time going through the moulting process, they are very hard to flush, and very difficult to kill.

In shooting woodcock by a cross shot, in July, August, and September, putting the gun forward on to their bills will be sufficient to bring them to bag: use at this season No. 9 or No. 10 shot. But in October, when they are on their strong migratory flight, supposing them to be forty yards distant from the gun, sight it some six inches forward of their long bills, which are always prominent marks. In both cases keep the gun moving even after it is discharged. At the latter season, use No. 9 shot. In November it is well to use No. 8, for the sportsman, while hunting for woodcock, will often find quail and partridge; and an old cock-partridge, at this time, will need shot of this size in order that the work may be sure.

The Period of Moulting.

Woodcock begin to moult or shed their feathers about the middle of August; and those who kill them about the last of August, or early in September, will find them queer-looking birds, — bob-tailed, from having lost their tail-feathers, and, as some sportsmen say, quite seedy. A part of the moult, which comes from them at this season, somewhat resembles Indian meal, and may be observed when they are shaken. They have at this time an odor peculiar to the moulting process, and of course are not quite so good to eat as at other times. While moulting, they make short and rapid flights, without the ordinary sharp ring, which is supposed to be given forth from the tip-end of their wing-feathers.

It is a wonder what becomes of the cocks at the moulting season. The question has often been asked by those who have most frequently hunted them, but has never been satisfactorily answered. Although in July the hunting-grounds may be full of them, at the moulting season they are very scarce; and though you may search in every variety of ground, you will never find them in large numbers. I have occasionally discovered a few during this period among the vines and briers, where at such times they are to be found, if found at all, and have noticed where, in these places, they have rubbed off their tail and other feathers. Generally, so thick is the network of underbrush, vines, and briers, — almost like a hedge, — at these places, that your dog must have good courage to force himself in. A pointer will be likely to back out altogether; or if he does go in, you may occasionally hear a short cry from him when the thorns prick him.

How the sharp ring is produced.

The opinion held by many sportsmen, that woodcock make their peculiar ring with the tips of their wing-feathers in flying, I do not entirely agree with. I am inclined to think that the *ring* is simply the utterance by the bird of a sharp cry when startled; and the fact that they do not make this noise at the moulting season is not, in my opinion, sufficient evidence that the sound is not thus produced. I believe that the withholding of the sound at this time arises more from indirect natural causes, incident to and connected with their change of feathers. Just as the barn-yard fowl at the time of incubation acts in a quiet, unnatural manner, and usually goes through a partial moulting process, from her long confinement to the nest.

I once had a good chance of testing this matter fully. While hunting woodcock one day, my dog pointed, and at the command "Go," dived into the tall grass where the cock had taken shelter from an October frost. Not seeing the bird rise, I supposed the dog must have come upon a rabbit instead. But, after a little tussle in the grass and briers, Dash appeared with a large woodcock in his mouth, which he brought to hand, and which I took from him unharmed. Having no conveniences for keeping the bird through the day, I wrung his neck. Had I thought to cut off the end feathers from his wings and let him fly, afterwards shooting him, I might have settled the question in a practical manner.

American and English Woodcock.

The American woodcock are much smaller than the English, averaging about one third less in size and weight. The English bird averages some twelve ounces in weight, while the American is seldom found to exceed eight or nine ounces. I once killed an American cock, which was, to all appearance, twice as large as any that I had ever before shot : and I have, in the course of my experience, killed a good many. Hanging by the neck he looked nearly as large as a young partridge two-thirds grown. I did not weigh him, but showed him to several old sportsmen, who thought him a veritable wonder, double the size of the ordinary American bird.

The nest of the English cock contains four eggs, which are of a dull white color with brown spots. Some English writers state that they have positive knowledge that the mother bird will carry away her young when danger threatens, as well as take them from dry lying-up places to soft feeding-grounds, and back again. If true, these are quite remarkable characteristics, especially when we consider the size and weight of the birds.

Scandinavian Woodcock.

Throughout Scandinavia woodcock are found in plentiful numbers. In Sweden and Norway they are extensively hunted, and their habits and characteristics have been in many respects carefully noted. The variety found in these countries differs in its habits somewhat from the English and American varieties, while it is much larger than the American bird and about the size of the English. According to Mr. L. Lloyd, in his work on the game-birds of Northern Europe, its usual length is fourteen inches, the expanse of its wings two feet and one inch, and its weight from twelve to fourteen ounces.

Varieties of woodcock are not uncommon in Sweden and Denmark. In these countries they are frequently found of a yellowish-white color, or with the head and wings white, or with white spots on the head and wings; and sometimes they are found entirely white. They sometimes resort to regions of high elevation, and have been found in districts at least 3,800 feet above the level of the sea.

It has been noted as a peculiarity of the Scandinavian bird, that, in the morning and evening during the spring and summer, prior to going to its feeding-grounds and returning to cover, it always flies several times backwards and forwards over precisely the same line of country. These flights often extend to a distance of seven miles and occupy about a quarter of an hour each way. It is generally admitted that these flights are connected with, or peculiar to, the pairing season, inasmuch as during autumn and midwinter they are not continued.

During the morning and evening flights the bird gives utterance to a peculiar call-note, which sportsmen express by knort, knort, knisp, or pisp. The knort is a hollow, coarse, and somewhat lengthened nasal sound; the knisp a short, fine, and sharp sort of whistle, which, when one is accustomed to it, may be heard at a distance. This note clearly appears to be one by which the betrothed invite each other to pairing, for the bird seems to pay but very little attention to the *knort*, but always listens and looks about as soon as it hears the *knisp* or *pisp*.

When the male and female woodcock meet in their flights, or come near each other, they chase one another, and cast themselves with the rapidity of lightning among the trees and bushes to the ground, and give quick and hurried utterance to their finer note of *pisp*. Although one can seldom witness actual pairing, it is certain that these actions are preparatory to the matrimonial act, and are to be looked upon as an evidence of the modesty with which the female bird meets the bold advances of her lover, for when the pairing season is over, one not unfrequently observes the male and female birds meeting without pursuing one another.

The Scandinavian woodcock is also an early breeder. It pairs in the spring; the female makes the nest, a mere bit of moss or heather hollowed out under a bush or tussock, and lays three or four eggs of a dirty yellow-green color, marked with large and dark brown spots, pretty equally distributed over the surface. They are one inch in length and one inch and four lines in thickness. This bird breeds but once a year, and its young are usually hatched about the end of May.

The mother, as with the partridge, and some other

birds, is very careful of her nest and young. When a dog or other animal approaches them, she conducts herself in such a manner as to lead him to suppose that she is wounded, until at such times she has succeeded in luring him to a distance from her brood or nest, when she gives him to understand that she has the free use of her members.

When her progeny are in danger she not unfrequently, it is said, removes them to a place of safety. Mr. Lloyd relates an instance of a sportsman shooting a woodcock flushed by the dogs, at about six feet from the ground, that was bearing an unfledged young one in her claws. The old bird grasped the young one with her feet, one foot having hold of one wing, and the other foot the other. From what Mr. Lloyd further says on this point, it seems to be pretty generally admitted among the sportsmen of his country that woodcock do possess the power of carrying their young about from place to place; and this testimony would seem to confirm the truth of a similar statement previously made with reference to English woodcock.

According to Mr. Lloyd, the migratory flights of woodcock are believed to be always nocturnal. No one, at least, either in England or Scandinavia, seems to have witnessed them in the daytime, and it is also the general belief that the migratory flights of these birds are pretty much confined to moonlight nights. But he adds: "This can hardly be the case, because an indefatigable sportsman tells us that, in the year 1845, these birds arrived in Scandinavia between the 29th of March and the 10th of April, when the nights were the darkest."

The oft-repeated fact of woodcock destroying themselves on dark nights, by flying against the windows of light-houses, goes very far to prove the correctness of this assertion.

It is the commonly received opinion in Scandinavia, that the woodcock when migrating always flies, as a rule, "*with the wind.*"

The woodcock is the only bird allowed to breed undisturbed, in certain districts in Scandinavia. "As with the owl, it is looked upon as a bird of ill omen, and when people hear its call-note at the pairing season, they lose heart, believing it to be a Troll-fogel, or bewitched bird ; and this simply, because on alighting on the ground it runs rapidly and unperceived from the spot.

"This strange feeling has not only the effect of deterring people from pursuing or injuring it, but causes them to entertain for it both fear and aversion. Hence, if a boy finds a woodcock in a snare or trap, he not only kicks it away from him with his foot, but *spits three several times* after it, as also on the spot where it has lain, to free himself from the *fortrollning* or enchantment to which he might otherwise be subjected."

The proper charge for a gun, in woodcock-shooting, as previously described, is from 2¾ to 3 drachms of powder, and 1 to 1¼ oz. of No. 8 or 9 shot.

QUAIL-SHOOTING.

NORTHERN QUAIL. (*Perdix Virginianus.*)

THE habits of the quail, or Virginia partridge, are better understood in this country than those of many other kinds of game-birds, from the fact that almost every one who has used the gun in shooting small birds and squirrels has flushed them, and has noticed their long and rapid flights.

In their nature and manner of living they much resemble the northern partridge, or ruffed grouse, and are called by the former name in most of the Southern States, and in Europe. In speaking of the *quail*, we give him his true appellation as known in the New England States.

The quail is a hardy bird, of very rapid flight. In going from you, they generally fly in a straight line, and seldom, if ever, turn to the right or left. Unlike the woodcock, quail are rarely found singly. The male bird is quite a handsome bird, and is designated as the "whistler," and takes charge of the brood just as the barn-yard cock looks out for his family. Quail possess considerable cunning, and are hard to bring to bag. When a covey of them are flushed, they spring from the ground with a whir and with tremendous velocity in every direction, like sparks from the blacksmith's hammer, and so suddenly that, unless the sportsman is well nerved up to the work they will get out of sight before he can bring his gun to his shoulder. They seldom fly unless started by fright; and when on the ground, the male bird leads off his family in the shape of a triangle. They are usually found about the headlands of fields of wheat, rye, corn, or buckwheat in the fall season, particularly in fields of the latter, which is their favorite food. But they are more often flushed in the hedges, by the stone-walls and fences with brush and grass headlands than elsewhere, as they return to these places from their venture into the fields at the first approach of danger. They will not stand for the dog in open field, unless there is some good cover for them. After being flushed, they generally scatter, and are found singly and in pairs, when they will lie to the dog, and can be bagged, one or two at a time.

When the hunter, after making several shots, cannot find his game again, if he have the patience to sit down quietly for half an hour at a short distance from his last shot, he will be pretty sure to hear the male bird calling his family together, and the scattered birds *peeping* as they answer and work up toward the *whistler.* The sportsman should then keep perfectly still, until he has reason to think they have had time to come together; and he should not try to imitate the cock's whistle, unless he be an expert, for these birds are wary, and can tell pretty surely whether or not it is a quail that is whistling.

Perhaps no bird flies more rapidly, all circumstances considered, than the quail; and the sportsman must be on the *qui vive* to get in both barrels effectively after the bevy have sprung; and also he needs a smart shooting gun, one capable of bringing down a bird at forty yards, as his second bird will frequently be at this distance. As a general thing, however, the sportsman gets quite near the quail; otherwise, they would be very scarce in the market. Quail seldom take to the tree unless much frightened, and then more generally in rough, mountainous countries, than in low meadow grounds. Their flight is often very long. It is said that they take in their flight but one respiration, which indicates that they possess great lung capacity. They will often keep up their flight for quite a distance after receiving their death-wound, dropping dead suddenly when under full headway in the air.

Quails usually make their nests on the ground, by the headlands of cultivated fields, among a few trees, and near a fence, or amidst tufts of grass. The number of eggs is from fifteen to twenty-four. Seventeen is the largest number I have ever seen in one nest.

This bird and the ruffed grouse are generally thought to be untamable.

I was in a hayfield one summer, when some farmers, in mowing, came across a quail's nest containing seventeen eggs. I persuaded them to leave a bit of grass standing about the nest, in order that it might not be disturbed, and that we might have an opportunity of watching the operations of the old quail. It was at the end of the field, and near an old fence. I was particularly desirous of seeing the young ones when they first came out of the shell; and, as I suspected it was about time for them to make their appearance, I kept a pretty close watch of the nest. One morning one of the men, in turning some hay near the nest, accidentally struck the old quail on the bill with the tine of his fork. She paid very little attention to this assault upon her, manifesting not the slightest disposition to move on. I was struck at once with this peculiar trait in a bird usually so very wild; and I began to poke her gently to see if she could be induced to leave the nest. I found that nothing but force would remove her, and so I left her, reflecting in my own mind upon Nature's wise provision in endowing so simple and so frail a creature with such a courageous and motherly instinct. On going to the nest the next morning I found it empty. The old bird had made off with her whole brood, and not one chick could I find. It then became apparent what made the old bird stick to her nest so courageously the day before, — she was about to leave it with her young ones, and did not want to let us know it. It is often quite amusing to see the uneducated sportsman try to find the young peepers, when only two or three days old, although he may have seen the whole covey alight but a short distance before him. The probabilities are that, after a tedious hunt, he will give up without finding the first one. During this chase the old cock will most likely be cutting up his pranks, running about as if with a broken wing, and luring the tyro away from the locality of the brood, which madame quail is meanwhile working off in another direction. It is wonderful to see the sagacity and tact exhibited by this bird and the partridge while rearing their brood, and to see with what astonishing quickness every chick disappears when any sudden danger comes.

In warm summer evenings you will often hear the old cock whistling from the top of a fence or high rock. His whistle is said by farmers to give the words " more wet " ; and it is certainly a very sweet note, and very difficult to imitate well.

The quail has many enemies, the fox, the mink, the weasel, and other animals. At night they roost in a circle on the ground, with their heads outward, in order to be on their guard against their foes. But their greatest destroyer, — one which often kills them by wholesale, — is the heavy snow in cold winters. For the quail is not entirely a migratory bird, like the woodcock. They do not give up in an ordinary snow-storm, although entirely covered, but will manage to work up through pretty deep snow, if it be new and light. But heavy and continued snow-storms, like those of the winter of 1866 – 67, often cover them too deeply for them to get out ; and when the snow is followed, as is frequently the case, by a light rain, it is likely to freeze and form a crust through which they cannot work. I have heard that many coveys of quail were found in the spring of 1867, which had been entirely frozen to death in this manner.

As previously mentioned, the quail should be hunted about the hedges of fields of grain, near copses of woods, and the low thick underbrush which forms their cover. If it be a dry season, work in lower ground, and *vice versa*. Their best feeding time is quite early in the morning. When the weather is wet or misty, however, they will feed much later in the day, working out into the open field as soon as the weather clears up a little. During rainy weather they will keep to the cover most of the day, not coming out till toward sunset, when the sportsman can almost always find them feeding ; but, as they are lively eaters, on good feeding-ground they will soon fill themselves.

I consider the quail the best game-bird with which to train the setter or pointer, as they give off a strong scent, and are likely to be found in open fields and among hedges, where the dog has a better chance to work under the care and direction of his master. The dog always loves the scent of this bird, and it is often difficult to keep him in, especially when on the trail of a whole covey.

When your dog is on the point for quail, walk up firmly but slowly until you get your position, and when all is ready, if your movements do not flush the covey, (as they often will) let the dog put them up, or put them up yourself according as the dog has been trained. After having discharged both barrels (which should be done by selecting a single bird at each shot), do not rush up yourself to bring in the game, neither let your dog do so ; but keep perfectly cool, and load where you stand, and as soon as possible, for there may be half a dozen birds within ten yards of you. When you have reloaded, let the dog bring in the dead birds, keeping him at the same time under control, and not letting him range all over the ground. After having emptied both barrels, cast your eye in the direction the game went ; watch sharply, and you will see them scaling along over fields and meadows, and when they begin to settle, watch closely, and you will have another shot at them. As they finally draw down to the ground, you will always notice that they give a sudden tip to their wings, — a movement that differs quite perceptibly from their regular flight, and which they have in common with nearly all kinds of game birds. Mark well then the spot when they come to the ground, by noting some big tree or rock in its vicinity; calculate well the distance, and make tracks for it directly, before losing your points of compass.

As previously stated in the rule given for woodcock shooting, a good marker will always have a better bag than the sportsman who has no faculty that way.

Quail often come into the farmers' barn-yards during severe winters, to pick up such hay-seed as they can find ; and if unmolested, they will hang around the barn all winter.

It is generally supposed by ornithologists, that these birds are partially migratory, going from their homes to the seaside during the hot weather, like people of fashion, and returning to their breeding-grounds before the first fall of snow. Some interesting statements have been made by those who have examined this question, and it is a fact, that large flocks of quail are sometimes found in hot, dry seasons, running on the ground in the vicinity of and toward the salt water, and so rapidly that a sportsman cannot keep pace with them. At such times they are uncommonly wild, and will not suffer a dog to point them. This fact that they are often found in large numbers about the salt water in hot weather, added to the fact that at such times they are quite scarce inland, gives support to the partially migratory theory.

In shooting these birds in the fall season, No. 8 shot should be used, with a full charge of powder; for most of the shots will be made in their rear, and their vulnerable parts will not be exposed. If your gun weighs about seven lbs., shoot 3 drachms of good powder, and $1\frac{1}{4}$ oz. of No. 8 shot. In cross shots, put the gun from twelve to eighteen inches ahead, if they are thirty-five or forty yards distant.

The Northern quail (*Perdix Virginianus*) much resembles the English quail, both in its habits and in the color of its flesh. But it is nearly one third smaller than the latter bird, and is quite unlike it in its call or whistle.

The American quail has been exported to Europe, but, so far as I can learn, there has been no success in raising them; and, being somewhat dissimilar in disposition, they have not mixed with the English birds.

QUAIL-SHOOTING.

In some portions of the Southern and Western States, quail are often found in such numbers, that large quantities are easily taken by driving them into traps or nets. In New England, however, they are not so plentiful; still in some seasons many are caught by the pot-hunters. A friend told me not long since of a very remarkable streak of luck he had on one occasion, when hunting these birds. Knowing where a trap was placed of the kind called a figure four, he approached it cautiously, and in doing so, discovered huddled together underneath it a whole bevy of quail. His first impulse was to blaze away at them; but not wishing to take advantage of their defenceless condition, his ready wit suggested a better plan than killing them outright. Accordingly, he shot away the standard that supported the trap, when down came the cover, enclosing the whole lot, — some thirteen good-sized birds. My friend assured me, this was the only time he ever bagged so many quail at one shot, and that, too, without drawing blood or starting a feather.

In some years the immense numbers of those birds that make their autumnal migration from Europe to Africa are incredible. It is recorded that on one occasion such a quantity of them appeared on the western coast of the kingdom of Naples, that one hundred thousand were taken in a single day, and all within the space of six miles: and on the island of Capri, not far from the city of Naples, so many are annually captured, that they form the principal source of the revenue of the Bishop of that diocese, who in consequence rejoices in the title of the Bishop of Quails.

Quail withholding their Scent.

It is an established fact, well known to the experienced hunter, that the quail and some other game-birds have the power of withholding their scent, — a power which they especially use in times of apparent danger. When making their last movements at evening to prepare for their roost, the quails fly to their roosting-places, and remain through the night without running about to leave a scent for foxes, weasels, and other hostile night animals. And this fact clearly shows that they know they have a scent, and that they can withhold it when safety requires. Every sportsman who has frequently hunted quail has had proof of this assertion, and has wondered why, even with a good pointer or setter, he could not find or flush the birds which he so recently saw alight on the very ground over which he has hunted. I have often observed, that not only quail, but woodcock, instead of running a short distance, as usual, will at times alight and lie up, as it is called; and the dog will work within a few feet of them without scenting them.

In this connection I will add an interesting statement, which will corroborate the foregoing, taken from Lewis's "American Sportsman," and written by Samuel B. Smith, M. D. Dr. Smith says: —

"How long has it been observed, and with regret, by sportsmen, that the best dogs could not discover certain birds of value, such as partridges (quail), in places where they were seen to settle themselves. And yet years have rolled away without a single individual advancing the only rational idea of the proper cause. The truth never reached them that these persecuted little creatures had been granted the power of withholding their odor to preserve them from their ruthless destroyers. Noble dogs have been censured as wanting and careless, when the often-repeated fact in almost every day's hunt made it manifest that the fault did not lie with them. Many years ago I noticed this fact, and, after frequent and earnest observation, I adopted the conclusion already given."

"It is now twenty years since I was one day in company with my friend and companion, the late learned ornithologist, Alexander Wilson, assisting him in his endeavors after the birds of this country. We encountered a well-appointed party of gentlemen who were shooting partridges [quail]. They had seven dogs, apparently of the best quality. They were in a large stubble-field, having small patches of low bushes and briers in several places. From one of these was flushed a very large covey of partridges, which, after having been rigorously fired upon, settled nearly in the centre of the field, in a place slightly depressed, where the stubble was unusually high, with rank clover underneath."

"The sportsmen pursued with due caution, giving the proper instructions and ample time to the dogs. Some of the birds were put up and killed, but not near as many as had taken refuge there. After considerable search, the party left the ground. Why so few of the birds were roused puzzled me exceedingly; and I, in common with every one, *censured the dogs*. Immediately adjacent to the stubble was a body of open woodland, in which Mr. Wilson was several hours engaged in his usual ardent study into the habits and manners of a number of small birds sporting in it. On our return home we crossed the stubble directly past the spot where the partridges had been hunted by the sportsman. As we approached it, a bird flew up, and soon another and another until five went off. I expressed my surprise to Mr. Wilson, who dismissed the matter by supposing that the stronger scent from the feet of so many men had transcended that of the birds, and bewildered the dogs."

"In October, 1824, I became assured of the truth of my doctrine. I was then in company with five gentlemen, in a fine partridge country. We had eleven dogs (setters and pointers) of approved value."

"The party concluded to range a field or two before breakfast; but I did not go out with them. I soon heard rapid firing in a new cleared ground in sight of the tavern house. I hurried to join them. There was a small meadow-land and a little brook intervening between us. On the margin of this meadow stood a large pine stump, covered with running dewberry vines, and surrounded by small oak-shrubs. I was within sixty yards of it, and parallel to it, when two partridges came directly towards me across the meadow. Having but one barrel charged, I fired upon the nearest bird, and killed it. The other made a sudden dart from its line, and took refuge among the shrubs and briers about the stump. I had my favorite dog, and a very valuable pointer-bitch with me. Having recharged, I approached in guard upon the marked bird; but the dogs gave no point. This was the proper time to test my belief. I therefore called off the dogs, and waited till I had every one on the ground brought to the spot. This was done; but there was no intimation given that there was a bird near us. We left the ground without remark or explanation, and retired to breakfast. In an hour we took the field for the day. I requested the gentlemen to indulge me again by an advance upon the stump, leading the van myself with the pointer-bitch. She instantly pointed, and the other dogs backed her. The bird was flushed and shot. I now explained myself fully, and Mr. Edward Tilgham, well known to most American sportsmen, was greatly struck with it. He expressed great pleasure too at it, as he said it would save many valuable animals from unmerited censure. He told me that he had more than once noticed the same fact with pheasants and grouse. I think it highly probable that these birds are endowed with the same power."

I can only add that my experience fully confirms Dr. Smith's theory.

For quail-shooting, load the same as for woodcock-shooting : $2\frac{3}{4}$ to 3 drachms of powder and $1\frac{1}{4}$ oz. shot, using No. 9 in the early part of the season, and No. 8 for late shooting.

RUFFED GROUSE OR PARTRIDGE SHOOTING. (*Tetrao umbellus.*)

PARTRIDGE-SHOOTING is a specialty by itself, though in some respects analogous to quail-shooting; and the sportsman who thinks it an easy matter to fill his bag with these noble birds will be apt to find himself mistaken. The New-England partridge or ruffed grouse is, under all circumstances, the bird of all game-birds, and is sample work for a good shot. The sportsman, old or young, who can knock down his partridge surely, when a fair chance offers, and can bring him to bag, may be set down as a sportsman who can shoot anything that flies.

The sudden and unexpected manner in which this bird flushes, his tremendous whir and buzzing of the wing, — making a noise not unlike that of a bass-drum, and as loud as that made by a whole bevy of quail, while the oldest hunter often does not know where to look for him, makes him the standard of game-birds. It requires more nerve to kill him than any other game bird shot on the wing.

Like the quail, he makes in his flight a straightforward bee-line course, not to be mistaken; and the gun must be planted quickly and squarely upon him, and must be a powerful shooter, or the sportsman will shoot in vain. This noble bird should be called the "Cock of the Woods." He is wonderfully powerful on the wing, knowing, wary, and ever on the alert.

In different States, partridges differ in color and size; and the manner of hunting them is also varied. In some parts of New England, in the rough, heavy-timbered country, they take to the tree when flushed; and when the leaves are off, they can be killed without much labor. In all sparsely wooded countries and States, especially where the ground is level, they seldom take to tree, but continue their flight with tremendous velocity, dodging bushes and limbs of trees with incredible dexterity, and always coming out safe and sound from dense places through which it is often impossible for the hunter to look.

They are usually found, in warm autumn mornings, on the outskirts of wooded land lying open to the sun, adjoining a wheat or corn field, where they feed much like quail, retiring to the woods if disturbed. Towards the middle of the day, when it is warm, you will be likely to find them in the woods, in low ground, near some spring or small stream, where they drink, and often eat the roots of vegetables growing in the water. When a number of partridges are started, they will almost always fly in the same direction. If they are wild and will not lie to the dog, the hunter who has company and is acquainted with the ground, will do well to send his partner around ahead of the game several rods, so that when the dog and gun work up, there will be a good chance to get one or more shots.

When the dog makes game, it is generally known to be the partridge if his movements are straightforward and rapid before he comes to the point. The partridge will not let the dog point on him unless he is under good cover, and often then only at long distances.

Partridges are frequently caught in snares by farmer-boys and *pot-hunters*, who catch them for the sake of filthy lucre; and in many places they are in this way entirely run out. Snares are made as follows. A hedge-fence is constructed of small staddle-trees, in the woods by the hillsides, usually where wintergreen berries are found. The crevices in the hedge are filled with leaves, making a sort of brush wall about two feet in height. At intervals of about four feet a hole is left open, for the insertion of a snare made in the form of a hoop. A little path is made on each side of the hedge, for the partridge to run in, by removing the leaves with the hand. The hedge is often many rods long, and when a flock of partridges meet it, instead of trying to jump or fly over it, they prefer to trot along and try to run through the loop-holes, playing a kind of hide-and-seek game. The snares are so constructed that in running through the loopholes the partridge runs its head and neck into a slipping noose, which tightens the more the bird strains to get away. These hedges are visited every day or two by the pot-hunters, and at times they take a dozen birds from one hedge ; and they usually have more than one hedge to watch. This is an outrage alike on the bird and on the honest sportsman. I have never hesitated to make known my opinion of such proceedings, or to put my boot through any hedge, or tear up any snares found by me while hunting, whether set for partridge, quail, or rabbits. Give them an even chance, I say, and they will never be entirely run out. Legislators ought to exhibit the practice of snaring game-birds as neither honorable nor manly. The course allowed by our game-laws, of killing woodcock and other game so early in the season, will, in a few years, it is feared, be the means of destroying almost every species of game-bird that flies. This should not be allowed ; game-birds should be protected. But about this subject I shall have more to say in another place.

When the partridge takes to the green covered tree, he usually alights toward the top, and it will be strange if you see him on the tree, and it will be still more strange if you kill him when he flies. Probably no bird is harder to kill on the wing than the partridge as it flies from the top of a high tree. Should he take to the tree in the fall, when the leaves are off, if he is in range of your gun, keep quiet, and look out sharp. Perhaps you will notice on a low limb, or half-way up, what looks like a *knot* running up to a peak : that is the bird. Unless you are *posted* you will probably see him a dozen times without knowing him, he imitates the knot and crook so well. If you wait too long before shooting, or stir too much, you will notice that the knots on the tree are one less, and that your partridge is gone.

Partridges generally make their nests on the ground, in the woods, and on a hillside ; and in the management of their brood they closely resemble the quail. Like the quail, they have for enemies the foxes, weasels, and other animals that prowl about the woods at night.

On or before the first of May, the female bird leaves the company of the male, and goes to a secluded place in the covert to make her nest and lay her eggs. She generally selects a spot by an old partially-decayed stump of a tree, or a log of wood, where there are decayed leaves ; and by drawing a few of the latter together, she makes an open, careless nest, and lays from seven to twelve eggs. The eggs are of a yellowish white color, differing somewhat in different States. During the season of incubation, the male bird retires, and is not allowed by the female to approach the nest until the young birds are pretty well grown ; then he returns, and resumes his former position in the family.

Partridges are usually shot at from the rear, and it takes a heavy charge to bring them down. If the hunter notices a peculiar motion or twitch in the bird's tail-feathers, after having shot at him, — something like the motion of the lark in flying, he may be sure that the bird is struck. Whether he shows it or not, if he has been shot at within a fair range and with good-sized shot, it will be a good plan to follow along the course flown over for forty or fifty rods, as they will often fly that distance and then drop dead.

I well remember once going out at some distance into the open field, to find a woodcock which had flown out of the woods. In coming back to the cover I followed a stone-wall hedge, when up flushed an old cock-partridge. I covered him with my gun, and let fly. I could not perceive any change in his flight, for he kept up the rapid, straightforward movement; yet still I thought I ought to have dropped him. The next morning while looking for more woodcock in the same cover, I found all at once in front of me a dead cock-partridge. It immediately occurred to me that this might be the bird shot at yesterday, and I made for the stone-wall in the open field, which I found was in a straight line from where the bird lay. It had flown one breath of about forty rods, and dropped dead.

In the summer and fall the cock-partridge is often heard drumming, usually while standing on a log or stump in the woods. Old hunters formerly supposed that they struck their wings against the log. But it is now generally admitted that the sound is made by inflating the body with air, and striking the wings against the sides. The wings being concave, hold the air to the body, and by their rapid motion produce a hollow guttural sound, which, even when the bird is quite near, has the effect of a distant booming noise. This is supposed to be an amorous noise, which the bird makes by way of showing his mighty powers to his weaker sisters, much as the tom-turkey gives off a peculiar sound while strutting about and spreading his tail-feathers; or perhaps more like the barn-yard cock when he flaps his wings before crowing, making a noise which somewhat resembles that of the partridge at a distance, and would probably be still more like it if the cock's lungs were inflated with air. The noise made by the partridge is called "drumming," because the bird in making it begins by striking his sides at intervals, slowly at first, then gradually faster and faster, keeping excellent time until the sound becomes a regular roll, resembling the beat of a drum, and which in a still day can be heard at considerable distance.

In August, when the broods of this bird are about three fourths grown, the gunner can at times have grand sport, and generally will soon fill his bag. The young birds are much more tame than their parents, and fly more clumsily, but will often get up to a satisfactory speed.

The European partridges are larger than ours, and fly with much less velocity. They are much easier game to kill, from the fact that they are found in open turnip-fields, grain-fields, and hedges. Englishmen who come to this country and hunt our partridges, make at first but poor work, while the case is reversed when our sportsmen visit England.

Samuels, in his ornithology of New England, says that in severe winter weather these birds dive into the snow, to keep from freezing. I cannot vouch for this statement, but presume it to be correct. I have observed that, if frightened by being shot at, when the snow is new and soft, these birds will sometimes dive into it to conceal their bodies, in which position they are easily bagged.

The sportsman's success in shooting ruffed grouse or partridge is quite uncertain, as they are so wild and wary that, unless they are numerous and have plenty of good thick cover to hide in, they will not let the dog approach near enough for a point. Some dogs are specially trained for them, and can make a point at long distances. After being once flushed, they break up and scatter wildly, and it is very hard to find any of them again, as they make long flights. Unless they are hunted when the young birds are nearly grown, and before the brood is broken up, it hardly pays for the sportsman to hunt them as a specialty.

Partridges feed in the grain-fields, much like the quail, and also in the woods on wild grapes and whortleberries. In midwinter, when the ground is covered with snow, they live on alder and laurel buds, and at such times their flesh is somewhat bitter. Some imagine that at this season they are not wholesome food; but I have frequently killed and eaten them in winter, without experiencing any unpleasant consequences.

There are several varieties of ruffed grouse or partridges in the United States. The red-necked spruce (also called partridges) are found in the northern parts of Maine, New Hampshire, and Vermont. They are but little sought for by sportsmen. A few have found their way into the Boston market during the past winter, but they do not meet with a ready sale, being quite inferior to the ruffed grouse (*Tetrao umbellus*), both in size and quality. These, with the pinnated grouse (*Tetrao cupido*) of the Western prairies, commonly known as the prairie-chickens ; the sharp-tailed grouse, found sparsely in Pennsylvania ; and the great sage grouse, found in the vicinity of the Rocky Mountains, comprise about all the varieties found in this country.

The names of ruffed grouse in the different States are as follows : —

Partridges, in the Northern and Eastern States.
Pheasants, in the Middle and Southern States.
Grouse, in the Western States.

The latter, however, is a different species of bird from the Northern ruffed grouse, and differs in its habits, living in the open prairies, away from wooded cover and running streams, while the ruffed grouse loves to dwell among the rocks and wooded hills.

In shooting this game as a specialty, I would recommend a gun weighing from $7\frac{1}{2}$ to 8 lbs. Use $3\frac{1}{2}$ drachms of powder, and $1\frac{1}{2}$ oz. shot. In August and September No. 7 shot will do, but in the autumn use No. 6.

PINNATED GROUSE, OR PRAIRIE-HEN.
(*Tetrao cupido.*)

THIS bird is confined in its habitat almost entirely to the Southern States and the plains of the great West. It delights in making its home in the open prairies, away from the running brooks and the shade and cover of trees, dark vales or high projecting rocks.

This variety of grouse is hunted in precisely the same manner as the ruffed grouse, with setter and pointer dogs. But these dogs are subjected to great hardships in pursuing this game, and the former particularly, as their long-feathered hair, so full and thick, soon heats them to such an extent that they suffer greatly for want of water, which is not found where the pinnated grouse live. In fact, it is generally believed that this bird does not drink at all, but sips in the dew and rain-drops from the grass and other objects with their bills.

These birds are wary and uncertain. To make anything like a fair bag of them they must be hunted with well-trained and hardy dogs, capable of enduring long-continued thirst. They must also be hunted at the right season, with wind and weather favorable. They are very hardy birds, and the gun must shoot powerfully in order to kill them at long distances.

Sometimes they are so wild that the sportsman cannot come within less than rifle-range of them before they take to the wing.

The Eastern setter or pointer cannot stand the hunt on the plains like the native dogs. The suffering from the hot winds is excessive, and the sportsman is often obliged to carry out water by horse and wagon for the use of his dogs. The hard labór attending this sport makes it so tedious that many hunters do not long continue it.

Of late years our Eastern markets have been well supplied with this game from Arkansas, Wisconsin, Iowa, and some other Western States. It comes in abundance late in the fall and in the winter, when it is frozen and packed, into barrels and sent by railroad. So plenty have these birds lately been in our Boston market that I have purchased them for seventy-five, and even for fifty cents per pair. A large number are brought from Iowa, where they are caught in nets and traps. These come to the market in better condition than those that have been killed with the gun. The meat of these birds is quite dark, and does not relish like that of the ruffed grouse of the Eastern States. The pinnated grouse weighs from three to three and a half pounds, and is easily domesticated ; while the ruffed grouse, on the other hand, is supposed to be, like the quail, completely untamable.

In order to make fair work in shooting this game, the gun should weigh about eight pounds, be of twelve bore, well balanced in hand, and should be loaded with $3\frac{1}{2}$ drachms of powder, and $1\frac{1}{2}$ oz. of No. 6 or 7 shot.

WILSON'S SNIPE. (*Scolopax Wilsonii.*)

THIS migratory bird is well known in this country, and is also found in other parts of the world. It is much sought for by epicures, being by some preferred to the woodcock.

Snipe make their appearance in the New-England States about the first of May, coming from the South in pairs, and can then be found in their marshy feeding-grounds, which are their temporary homes, before they wisp themselves off to Canada, or other northern breeding-places.

Many localities afford fine shooting of these birds in the fall and spring; and as snipe are a kind of go-between for inland shooting, coming on in the spring before any other game-bird can be shot, and often remaining quite late in the fall, they furnish, in the proper localities, and under certain circumstances, very excellent sport.

Snipe, however, are very uncertain birds to find. With favorable weather, and at the proper season, the gun can be made lively; while at other times, with the best apparent prospect of filling the game-bag, nothing but their chalks and borings can be found.

The Wilson snipe is a bird of very rapid flight, and is capable of making as many, if not more, curves and angles on the wing, than any other game-bird which the sportsman follows. Especially is this true in cold, clear, windy weather.

When they arrive from the South, they are always wild, and constantly vacillating from one ground to another; and this uncertainty is very discouraging to the sportsman, unless he has excellent feeding-grounds near him.

The rule for snipe-shooting is to beat down wind while hunting, if the nature of the ground will permit. If possible, it will pay the hunter well to travel to the extremity of his ground, in order to take advantage of this fact, as the snipe almost invariably rise to windward. But if this cannot be done, the hunter must compromise by working in an oblique direction. When the dogs are on a point, always make it a rule to have the bird to leeward of you; that is, to have the wind blowing on your back; it will much increase your chance of success.

As with the woodcock, there is much judgment and alertness to be used in marking down this bird, after he is flushed and has gone off on his zigzag movements. Sometimes, after doubling and sailing away almost out of sight, he will come back and drop within a dozen feet of his starting-point.

A good, steady setter is the dog for this business, although many sportsmen prefer the pointer. But I have noticed that the latter dog seems to suffer more from the cold wind, and sometimes flatly refuses to enter the water, which is seldom the case with the setter dog.

These mud-paddlers are so irregular in their movements, and are so much governed by the state of the atmosphere, that they are discouraging game even for the most experienced sportsman. The uncertainty of finding them, and the certainty of finding plenty of mud and water, — the prospect of going home shivering with cold, with your dog in the same condition, and an empty bag to boot, — makes this kind of sport hardly endurable, except under rarely favorable circumstances. This unpleasantness is the rock upon which so many snipe-shooters have split.

On rising, snipe almost always hang for a couple of seconds before starting on their irregular course. Many writers and sportsmen claim that this is the nick of time for dropping them. But on this point there are many conflicting opinions. Some declare that they fly immediately after being flushed, and that the sportsman must wait until the zigzag course is over; while others assure us that if we were to do so, we should seldom or never have a shot. From my own experience, and from the testimony of others who have made snipe-shooting a specialty, I am inclined to believe that these birds do not conform in their flight to any rules, and that they indulge in all the eccentricities which are commonly charged to them. But whatever the changes in their manner of flying may be, the sportsman will soon learn their tricks, and be able to drop them at the proper time.

In shooting snipe, the gun should be put well ahead on the cross shots, or the shot will go behind. The quick and eccentric manner the snipe has of doubling over as he takes the ground is remarkable and amusing. The novice will at first make poor work, both in shooting and marking down this bird. It is noticeable that while some sportsmen can easily drop their Wilson at almost every shot, they will about as often miss their woodcock or quail; with this exception, however, in their favor, that the former bird is usually killed in open shooting, the reverse being the case with the other game. Almost every sportsman has his favorite game-bird to shoot, and the very fact that he thinks he is sure to kill gives him confidence and success.

The snipe in the spring is usually poor, but is in fine condition in the fall. I shot a number last fall that were almost as large as medium-sized woodcock; and in the autumn they much resemble the latter bird. In windy days these birds lie closer than in mild, calm weather, and the dog can make more points at such times. But they are more difficult to kill when the wind is fresh, as their flight is then much more rapid. When they have been followed long, even in mild weather, they will not stand well to the point, and they make wild and extended flights.

Their sense of hearing is very acute, and, unlike the woodcock, they will not often let the setter or pointer make very close visits. On this account it sometimes happens that, when snipe are abundant, the sportsman, in company with a friend, can make a larger bag, and with greater ease, by leaving his dogs Dash and Trip at home, than by taking them with him.

This bird is a remarkable barometer, for at about

every change in the atmosphere he makes a shift in his locality.

Wilson's snipe are very abundant in Canada and the northern part of New England, during their breeding time. As with the woodcock, their nests are made in the rudest manner, being nothing more than a hole in thick grass, and perhaps eked out with a few of their own feathers. The number of eggs is four, from which they are usually successful in rearing four young long-bills. The young ones are soon able to do some boring in a small way, in the softest and most tender feeding-grounds, to which they are convoyed by the old birds.

It has been stated (I cannot tell with how much truth) that formerly, when an English nobleman wished to test the capacity and endurance of his new game-keeper, he would send him into a snipe-bog, to hunt and wade for a few days in the mud and mire. If he came out without colds or rheumatism, he was considered hardy enough for any emergency.

Snipe shooting-grounds are generally discovered by accident while hunting for other game, and they are usually located in low, swampy land, without many trees, and where the water from the small streams overflows the meadows. Generally such ground is partially covered with bogs and long grass, and numerous little islands with small bushes, surrounded with coarse rank grass; and as the water recedes it leaves the ground in fine condition for boring.

All such meadows, however, are not good snipe ground by any means, for there are thousands of acres of such land where a snipe would not consent to stay over night. While, again, there may be others apparently inferior which may be favorite feeding-places, and where game may always be found, if found at all.

Usually the sportsman who follows this game has some choice places that are not generally known, and, visiting them at the proper times, he will not unfrequently be paid for his labor. But, at the best, it is uncertain sport; and the seasons will often come and go, when these birds will be so scarce, that the sportsman will not take the trouble to hunt over his own grounds.

If the young sportsman knows of good snipe shooting-ground, and wants to know if they are about, without the trouble of hunting his grounds over, his best way is to watch the market, if living near one, as snipe, if plenty, will pretty surely find their way there.

I add an interesting story related of a tame snipe:—

"A gentleman of Chatham, N. J., while snipe-shooting on the excellent meadows there, last September, shot a snipe, or at least knocked it down. After all was ready, he told the dog to "go find dead bird," which the dog did in excellent style, and retrieved it without hurting it in the least. In taking it from the dog's mouth it was seen to be uninjured, except a slight scratch on the head, which had evidently only stunned it, for as soon as it was taken out of the dog's mouth it was lively enough to have flown away again if it could only have got at liberty. The gentleman took the bird, put grass all around it, and, taking the napkin off his lunch, wrapped the bird up in it very carefully, so that it could not get hurt in his pocket. He continued hunting, but only getting three brace he returned home, rejoicing over the capture of a live English snipe. Arriving home, he took the bird out of his pocket, and put it on the floor. It immediately commenced hopping around and feeling of everything with its long bill, and seemingly took great pleasure in standing in front of the fire on one leg, with its bill under its wing.

"It never showed any signs of fear, and might well have been called a game bird. It would allow the dogs to point it, and took great delight in being petted. Holding a worm in your fingers, so that it could be seen, the bird would come running up to get it, and then, hopping away to a pan filled with water, would there wash the worm and then swallow it. After taking a little drink it was all ready for another worm. The bird washed itself every morning, but wanted fresh, clean water every time, as it would never wash in the same water twice. Its chief amusement was boring, which it did in a large milkpan filled with mud, grass, and worms. It would eat more than twice its own weight of worms each day. Its owner watched it for three hours, and in that time it consumed seventy-one worms. The gentleman afterwards got seventy worms, and found them to weigh five ounces, while the snipe weighed but three ounces. It was generally a very lively and wakeful bird, although at times it would go to sleep in your hand. But with all the eating the bird did, it kept continually getting thinner and thinner, and after nearly two months' captivity it died. It evidently must have died of starvation, for it was so poor at last you could almost see through it. Its natural food must have been something besides worms. In its appearance it was one of the handsomest birds ever put in a cage."

In shooting these birds, use the woodcock gun of $6\frac{1}{2}$ to 7 lbs. weight, using Nos. 8 or 9 shot, according to the season, and making the charge the same as for woodcock, i. e., $2\frac{3}{4}$ drachms powder to $1\frac{1}{4}$ oz. of shot.

BAY SHOOTING.

THE shooting of birds known as *not true game*, in our bays, in and about the creeks of our harbors, and in salt marshes, has of late years been so uncertain that I have paid little or no attention to it. I made my last trial two years ago, and gave it up as a kind of hunting I could find but little pleasure in. Several of my acquaintances who have followed it in its season as a specialty have the past few years been so unsuccessful as to lead them to discard this kind of shooting altogether, on our New England coasts. I know one sportsman who, last summer, went some distance and spent two months in hunting bay birds, but came home quite disgusted, having made no bag at all. Sportsmen who are conveniently located in their homes for watching the shooting-grounds for all kinds of marsh-birds, and who take hold at the right time, in a season of good flight, occasionally have fair luck. And in some of the Southern and Middle States bordering on the Atlantic, sportsmen often find splendid shooting among various kinds of shore birds, as they migrate North or return to their feeding-places at the South. But the killing of these birds is ruled out from the order of regular shooting. At the best it is wearisome and dirty work, and the crack shot soon tires of it. Almost any boy who can fire a gun can kill some from a flock of these birds, when they come to the stool. A good sportsman finds more pleasure in knocking over a pair of woodcock or a brace of quail, than in bagging a dozen marsh birds at one shot, in their oozy, swampy grounds. There is nothing elegant or artistic, to my mind, in bay shooting, — nothing to make such shooting other than mere slaughtering. Frank Forrester, in speaking of this kind of sport expresses my opinion of it precisely. He says:—

"To me, I confess, the sport is a dull one, weary, stale, unprofitable; and the only things that could reconcile me to it are the chance of obtaining rare and curious ornithological specimens, and admiration for the skill and imitative talents of the baymen. Sport to me in it there is little. If the birds are scarce, shy, and void the stools, the reek of the mud banks, and stagnant waters, interspersed with savory odors of departed king-crabs and such like, the blazing sunshine of an American May or June reflected from the smooth, heaving waters, and, above all, the torturing sting of the mosquitoes, are hardly compensated by a few scattering shots. If, on the contrary, the flocks come, as they do sometimes, countless in numbers and in quick succession, there is too much of it. It becomes butchery, not sport."

Give me brush shooting, instead of such unpleasant work and such uncertainty as attend all kinds of shooting for marsh birds.

The following are the names of some of the bay-snipe, as they are called, that visit our Atlantic coast, frequenting the creeks and marshes when making their migratory flights to the Northward in the spring, and when returning to their home in the South in the summer and autumn : —

BLACK-BELLIED PLOVER (*Charadrias apricarius*).

These shore-birds are better known in the Northern States than many other birds on our coast, where they make a short stay, and then hie away to the rolling grounds and uplands of almost every part of New England. They are shy and watchful birds, and hard to get within shooting distance. The baymen shoot them from stands, made generally by digging holes in the ground, as they do many other birds on our Atlantic coast. It takes strong shooting to bring them to bag. When on the uplands, they feed upon grasshoppers and other insects, and are very rapid on their pinions. In the summer months nearly all farmers' boys have some knowledge of the whereabouts of these birds, having seen them in the pastures and on large hills. They usually know them by the name of *kill-deers*.

WILLETT OR STONE CURLEW (*Scolopax semipalmata*).

The Willett belongs to the numerous snipe family. Its cry is shrill and peculiar, and when once heard is seldom forgotten. Sportsmen are always anxious to bag these birds. They build their nests in the marshes of the Northern States, and return to the South in October.

Red-Breasted Snipe.

This bird closely resembles Wilson's snipe in its fall and winter dress, but is dissimilar in its habits and in its flavor. The latter bird frequents fresh-water marshes, while the former is found in the low grounds and salt marshes along our coast. The red-breasts, moreover, congregate in large flocks, while the Wilson is mostly found alone or in pairs. The red-breasted snipe is known among baymen as the *Brown-back*, and is considered more delicious in flavor than any other sea-bird. But on account of its small size, sportsmen do not give so much attention to it as to larger game.

This bird is also known as the *quail-snipe*, and is migratory, returning from the North in large flocks, about the first of August. They are not so wary as most shore-birds, and the sportsman often kills several at one shot. They feed on snails and insects, which they pick up when the tide is receding. When in company with other birds, they can readily be distinguished by their color.

Clapper-Rail or Mud-Hen (*Rallus crepitans*).

The mud-hen or big rails are migratory birds, found along our seaboard as far down as South Carolina, and are especially plentiful in and about the marshes of Delaware Bay, and in the State of New Jersey. They are not considered very good eating. They are large, sluggish on the wing, and easily knocked down even by the novice sportsman. It is hard to make them take wing, as they depend for protection more upon diving and swimming than upon their flight.

ESQUIMAUX OR SHORT-BILLED CURLEW (*Scolopax borealis*), AND LONG-BILLED CURLEW, OR SICKLE-BILL (*Numenius longirostris.*)

The former is distinguished from other varieties as the jack-curlew. They migrate to their breeding-places at the North, and return in large numbers to their southern homes in September, at which time they are abundant in the vicinity of Delaware Bay. Their flesh is deemed of fair quality.

The long-billed curlew belongs to the Esquimaux variety, which it resembles in its habits and in its choice of a feeding-ground. Both varieties are killed from boats, or from stands made by digging holes in the ground. There is still another very similar variety, called the *Doe-bird*, which also rejoices in the name of jack-curlew.

But further details I leave to writers on Natural History. My object is accomplished when I have pointed out the prominent varieties to be met with by those who are in search of such game, which, as before observed, is not "true game."

WILD-FOWL SHOOTING.

WILD DUCKS.

WILD-DUCK shooting, embracing as it usually does, all kinds of wild-fowl shooting, is a very different sport from brush-shooting. It is attended with so many hardships and uncertainties that, unless the sportsman lives near the sea or some inland lake where the wild-fowl resort, it will hardly pay for him to leave the woods and fields, and seek water-fowl instead of his usual inland game. The time for shooting wild duck and other water-fowl is also the season when woodcock, quail, and partridge are plenty, as it is, in fact, the harvest season for all game-birds. Wild-fowl shooting is at best a tedious, wearisome business, and whoever puts on the harness to follow it must make up his mind for all kinds of disagreeable work. He will often suffer from cold winds, storms, and wet feet, and sometimes he will go home empty-handed.

The best season for shooting wild ducks is the fall, beginning with the first of October, and continuing until December, often, indeed, much later into the winter. If you live near a fresh pond or lake, you should prepare a shooting-blind or brush house, and visit it whenever you can, particularly on windy mornings and evenings. You would find it convenient to have

WILD-FOWL SHOOTING IN PONDS OR LAKES.

your brush house within about twenty yards of the pond, made by driving into the ground four stakes at the angles of a square, and connecting the same by a strip of wood for support. Then cut some small trees and bushes, sharpen the ends, and drive them into the ground, fastening them to the bars. If well done, it will make a good cover, and can easily be repaired when out of order. When done the whole should look like a low cluster of trees and bushes, and it should not have too much the appearance of a hut. Put on the floor a quantity of dry hay to sit upon. Make the house sufficiently high to stand in, so that if you are up and on the lookout when the fowl are coming in, you can quietly drop down again without being seen.

Set out in the pond good wooden or living decoys. The latter are preferable if they can be had, as they will call the wild ducks about them. Be careful how you move about in your shooting-stand when the ducks are in the pond or are coming in. They are very quick to notice a sudden movement; probably no bird or fowl of any kind can excel them in this. When they have come down to the decoys, and are within range of the gun, find some little open space in your brush house. Draw back your gun and put the muzzle to the hole, but not through it, lest your motions should be discovered. When you shoot, sight your gun down close to the water, to avoid shooting over. It is always safer, when on the lookout for ducks, to sit down, with your little port-holes all engaged in different directions.

If a number of ducks are in the pond, wait until they have come together, so that you can secure as many as possible, and endeavor to shoot at them while their sides and tails are towards you. It will be almost impossible to kill them when they first rise out of the water. I know of no fowl that rises from the water so quickly as the common black duck, and where they get their tremendous force and velocity it is difficult to imagine. After having discharged both barrels at the ducks on the water, you must reload as quickly as possible, and look out for the lively cripples, letting the dead fowl lie until the others are secured. If the cripples once get to the shore, they will soon hide themselves, and it will trouble you to find them. They will work into the smallest imaginable holes; and should you, while searching for them, notice the tip-end of a feather sticking an inch or two out of the ground, I would advise you to give it a pull, for you will probably find a good fat duck at the other end.

If your pond is situated near the salt water, you must visit it — day or night — when the tide is within about two hours of being full; for, as it comes in, it drives the ducks from the low salt-water marshes, and they then fly to the fresh-water ponds to wash and prune themselves. It is quite interesting to see them take their fresh-water baths. They make the water fly several feet into the air, and sail about with great rapidity.

During the months of October and November, wild-duck shooting on our Northern and Western lakes is exceedingly fine sport; and so attractive is it that many sportsmen from New York and the New England States go annually to these lakes, and make a business of shooting for the market. And a good business they make of it. Not only are they able to pay their expenses, but they generally derive considerable income beside ; and, added to these pecuniary results, they get a certain enjoyment which cannot be expressed in dollars and cents.

The varieties of ducks found on our Northern and Western lakes are quite various, and many of them are of exceedingly fine flavor. The mallard, the American widgeon, the black duck, and many others are found in great numbers. In the autumn, these ducks, having fed on the wild celery and other choice food abundant on our inland waters, are in very fine condition. The usual method of shooting these ducks is to take them at their places of rendezvous. These places are readily discovered. They are generally found in large bays or inlets, particularly in such as contain large patches of wild grass and celery.

Into these places the ducks come in great quantities, flying in about sunset, and leaving about sunrise. Sportsmen arrange to take them on these occasions. If evening sport be desired, sportsmen locate themselves with their boats and decoys in the most desirable and least observable positions, in the afternoon, before the ducks begin to arrive. The ducks are then taken as they come in ; and it not unfrequently occurs that the guns are kept in constant operation, and that one or two hours suffices to nearly load a boat with game. If morning sport be desired, sportsmen locate themselves before daylight, and then take the ducks as they start out.

Many wild ducks, and geese also, are killed in the ponds and lakes of nearly all the Northern States, on their passages to the North and South. In the fall season, however, the harvest is far the greatest, and the arrangements of the sportsmen are generally so well-contrived and carried out, that but few ducks or geese get away when once they come within range of the sportsman's gun.

The manner of shooting ducks or geese where the pond is large and the game abundant, is as follows: —

On the edge of a lake or pond, and in the most secluded part, where the ducks or geese would naturally come without fear of being molested, and where the bushes and trees make a good cover, sportsmen build a small house, large enough to accommodate half a dozen inmates. The roof of this house they usually cover with brush and evergreens, in such a manner that the building cannot be noticed by the wild fowl, either in flying over or in sailing about the lake or pond. Here the hunters often live for two or three months at a time.

A few feet from this building, they erect a kind of wall or blind, made of brush, small pine trees and underwood, by running poles from one tree to another horizontally, and then standing and fastening some small trees against the poles, and filling in the chinks between with small brush; all this, without giving to the wall a heavy appearance.

This blind is made a little higher than the heads of

the shooters, who, while sitting in their "cabin home" with the whole range of the lake before them, can discover at its extreme end the first appearance of any fowl.

Along this wall of brush, at convenient distances, are left little open port-holes, through which the hunters put their double-barrelled shot-guns to shoot. The sportsmen are so well covered and shaded by the leaves of the trees, and their blind, that this can be done without their being noticed by the game.

On the edge of the lake, fastened by a string, are placed live wild-geese decoys; and, at a short distance from these are placed the decoys for the wild ducks. Some distance out toward the middle of the lake is a row of wooden decoys for wild geese, looking quite natural, with their tall necks erect, and apparently on the *qui vive* for any danger.

If geese come into the pond, they generally alight near the centre, and take a view of their surroundings. After they have begun to feel a little at home in the lake, the sportsmen begin to draw in their wooden geese decoys toward the shooting-stand, and the wild geese will follow. The live decoys fastened at the water's edge usually give them a reception by calling and flapping their wings; and every inducement is offered for them to swim in toward the shore. At times, however, they are very wary, and it takes hours for them to work up within range of the guns.

At such times the hunters often adopt a plan, which some call "toling in," and others "the ball game." This consists in having a little hole made at the bottom of the hedge or blind, and rolling a ball through to the edge of the lake, for a little spaniel dog, trained to the work, to follow and bring in. The wild fowl are attracted by the dog's manœuvres as he frolics and jumps along the shore. Their curiosity once excited, they swim in to see what pleases the little animal so much. Meeting, as they do, the living decoys, they often come boldly within twenty yards of the shooting-blind, where the double-barrelled shotguns are ready to pour in upon them a heavy volley of shot, from which but few can escape. In such cases, each shooter has an extra double-gun, in order to pick up the wounded fowl, and, if possible, to get another shot at the others on the wing.

Some of the ducking parties, while on these hunts, employ their time in working at their trade of shoemaking. By having one of their company detailed to watch for wild-fowl a certain number of hours each day, relieved in turn by others, they are sure to be ready at the first call to shoulder arms. At such times, the lapstone and strap drop remarkably quick, and the attention of the whole party is directed to other business than that of making shoes.

CANVAS-BACK DUCK (*Anas vallisneria*).

This far-famed water-fowl of the wild duck species is exclusively a native of this country, and is justly celebrated on account of the delicious flavor of its flesh.

Canvas-back ducks are found in many of the Southern States, but their great habitat is in and about the Chesapeake Bay and the Potomac River. Here they find, by deep diving, quantities of a peculiar kind of wild celery; and it is claimed by many that it is this food which gives their flesh its fine flavor.

Canvas-backs are exceedingly difficult game to kill, as they are very shy and fly with great rapidity. When not mortally wounded they are very hard to gather up, as they will swim a long time under water, and exhaust the patience of almost any dog in following them.

The prices these ducks bring in the markets of the principal cities from Boston to New Orleans are such as to tempt many fowlers in pursuit of them for the mere purpose of gain; and the shooting of them in the above-named waters at the proper season is a business of no small magnitude. It is impossible to estimate the quantity of these ducks taken in a good season. I have heard of parties bringing away loads of them; and when we consider the great extent of territory embraced in the Chesapeake Bay and Potomac River district, and contemplate the peculiar adaptiveness of this territory for furnishing both sustenance and places of rendezvous for ducks, we need not be surprised at the reports which sportsmen bring of their operations there.

Canvas-back ducks can easily be detected from others, even at a great distance. In flying, their velocity is much greater than that of other varieties of ducks; and in the water they can readily be distinguished by their constant habit of diving.

The canvas-back is so noted a duck, that many sportsmen go annually from almost every part of the country to indulge in the rare sport of shooting this delicious game, and as the processes or devices employed in getting them within range are applicable to the hunting of almost every kind of duck in any part of the country, I will give briefly some of the "ways and means" used for this purpose. Dr. E. J. Lewis, in "The American Sportsman," a book full of valuable information respecting the habits and varieties of American game, has given in detail the various means employed both by the sportsmen and the pot-hunters in taking ducks in the Chesapeake and Potomac waters, and I cannot do better than to make some extracts from his account of the various devices employed for taking the canvas-back.

Toling Ducks.

Dr. Lewis describes this process as follows: —

"A species of mongrel water-dog, or often any common cur, is taught to run backwards and forwards after stones, sticks, or other missiles, thrown from one side to the other along the shore. In his activity and industry in this simple branch of education, within the comprehension of any dog, consists the almost incredible art of *toling* the canvas-back. With a dog of this character, the shooting party, consisting of several persons, all prepared with heavy double-barrelled duck-guns, ensconce themselves at break of day behind some one of the numerous blinds temporarily erected along the shore contiguous to the feeding-grounds of these ducks.

"Everything being arranged and the morning mists cleared off, the ducks will be seen securely feeding on the shallows not less than several hundred yards from the shore. The dog is now put in motion by throwing stones from one side of the blind to the other. This will soon be perceived by the ducks, who, stimulated by an extreme degree of curiosity, and feeling anxious to inform themselves as to this sudden and singular phenomenon, raise their heads high in the water and commence swimming for the shore. The dog being kept in motion, the ducks will not arrest their progress until within a few feet of the water's edge, and oftentimes will stand on the beach, staring as it were in mute and silly astonishment, at the playful motions of the animal.

"If well trained, the dog takes no notice whatever of the ducks, but continues his fascination until the quick report of the battery announces to him that his services are now wanted in another quarter; and he immediately rushes into the water to arrest the flight of the maimed and wounded, who, struggling on every side, dye the water with their rich blood.

"The discovery of this mode of decoying ducks was quite accidental, being attributed to a circumstance noticed by a sportsman, who, concealed behind a blind patiently awaiting the near approach of the canvas-backs, observed that they suddenly lifted up their heads and moved towards the shore. Wondering at this singular and unusual procedure on the part of this wary bird, he naturally looked round to discover the cause, and observed a young fox sporting on the river-bank; and the ducks, all eagerness to gaze upon him, were steering their course directly for the shore.

"These ducks will not only be decoyed by the dog, but will often come in by waving a fancy-colored handkerchief attached to the ramrod. We have seen a dog fail to attract their attention till bound around the loins with a white handkerchief, and then succeed perfectly well. The *toling* season continues about three weeks from the first appearance of the ducks, — often a much shorter time, as these birds become more cautious, and are no longer deceived in this way. The canvas-back toles better than any other duck; in fact, it is asserted by some sportsmen that this particular variety alone can be decoyed in this mode. There are always numbers of other ducks feeding with the canvas-back, particularly the red-heads and black-heads, who partake of the top of the grass which the canvas-back discards after eating off the root. These ducks, though they come in with the canvas-backs when toled, do not seem to take any notice whatever of the dog, but continue to swim along, carelessly feeding, as if intrusting themselves entirely to the guidance of the other fowl.

"As far as we have been able to judge, we are inclined to this opinion also, and do not recollect ever having succeeded in toling any other species of duck unaccompanied by the canvas-back, although we have made the effort many times. These ducks are a very singular bird, and, although very cunning under ordinary circumstances, seem perfectly bewildered upon this subject. We were one of a party several years since who actually succeeded in decoying the same batch of ducks three successive times in the course of an hour, and slaying at each fire a large number. We counted out over forty at the conclusion of the sport.

"Although the *toling* of ducks is so simple in its process, there are few dogs who have sufficient industry and perseverance to arrive at any degree of perfection in the art. The dog, if not possessed of some sagacity and considerable training, is very apt to tire and stop running when the ducks have got near the shore but too far off to be reached by the guns, which spoils all, as the birds are very apt to swim or fly off if the motion of the animal is arrested for a few moments."*

"Since writing the above, we have been assured by an experienced and somewhat veteran sportsman that both the black-heads and the red-heads tole with the same facility, and the former duck, if anything, even more easily than the canvas-backs. From further

---

* "On some particular days, even in the midst of the toling season, without any apparent reason, the toler is obliged to relinquish his sport, as no artifice on the part of the dog will induce the ducks to *come in*, although on the preceding day they may have exhibited the greatest eagerness to satisfy their curiosity on this point. The immediate cause of this fickleness on the part of these fowl it is difficult to explain, as it cannot be attributed to any sudden change in the weather or other concomitant circumstances which most generally influence the actions of the feathered race."

observation and more minute inquiry on the subject of *toling*, we are now inclined to think that very nearly all varieties of the wild fowl can be decoyed in the way above described; but at the same time we are more than ever convinced that the canvas-back is more susceptible to this strange influence than any other duck on our waters. The reason why we were at first led to suppose that the canvas-back alone could be influenced by these playful motions of a dog was owing to the circumstance of our never having at that time *toled* wild fowl on other waters than the Chesapeake, where the canvas-back is always to be seen feeding during the shooting season in company with all the other varieties that flock to this favorite resort; and we had not perhaps considered how seldom it was that a *bed* of ducks could be seen on these waters that did not chiefly consist of canvas-backs, as the most of the other varieties keep company with these ducks for the purpose of feeding on the refuse of the celery which *they*, by their superior strength and dexterity, are enabled to pull up from the bottom of the rivers. We consequently may have been perfectly correct in our assertion "*of never having succeeded in toling any other species of duck unaccompanied by the canvas-back*"; but at the same time our inferences may have been entirely wrong, when we consider how seldom a *bed* of ducks is seen on these waters that is not principally composed of canvas-backs. And, moreover, when we consider the acuteness of vision and the never-ceasing watchfulness of the canvas-back, we need not be at all surprised that they should be most generally the first to notice the dog or the first to take the lead in the general movement towards the shore, — all the other ducks apparently following, although they may be equally under the magic influence.

"This plan of killing ducks, though practised by all the gentry as well as pot-hunters who frequent the bay-shore, is not altogether recognised as a sportsmanlike way of bagging game, and is forbidden on some of the grounds in possession of the clubs that meet during the shooting season at different points in the bay. Against the utility of this regulation we will not venture an argument. The gentlemen composing these associations no doubt have good reasons for their restriction. We must confess, however, that we see no impropriety nor anything unsportsmanlike in thus decoying this wary fowl within reach of our guns, more particularly in positions where all other modes of getting at them would surely fail; but, on the contrary, we have always found a great deal in the sport to admire, as it is not unfrequently attended with a high degree of pleasurable excitement, while witnessing the playful antics of the dog operating so strangely upon his bewildered and silly victims that so soon pay the forfeit of their idle curiosity in death. And, moreover, if we desired to act the part of a sage, we might also draw a pretty moral from the incident, in demonstrating to our brother sportsmen that a foolish and idle curiosity even in the brute creation often results in disastrous consequences to the parties concerned.

"Along some shores on the Gunpowder and Bush Rivers, exclusively devoted by their proprietors to *tol-*

ing, the season for this sport continues very late, as the fowl are seldom or never disturbed upon their feeding-grounds far out in the stream, where they take immediate refuge after being fired at and remain in perfect security till enticed again within gunshot; and this may be accomplished several times during the same day, and the slaughter consequently is often enormous. This method of killing ducks is less injurious in its effects upon the movements of wild fowl than any kind of *boat-shooting* that can be practised, as it never disturbs them on their feeding-grounds, but attacks them only when foolishly wandering away from their usual secure haunts.

"The proper and most destructive moment to shoot ducks, when they have been toled, is when they present a side view.

"Duck-dogs, when behind the blinds along the bay-shore, mark the flight of wild fowl as anxiously as the sportsman himself, and often by their manner give evidence of the approach of ducks before they are observed by those on the watch for them.

Boating Ducks.

"Another method of killing canvas-backs is that of boating them on their feeding-grounds in small skiffs, either in the daytime or during the still hour of night. The latter plan, of course, is the most destructive and terrifying to the fowl.

"A large swivel, carrying several ounces of powder and a pound or more of shot, is placed on the bow of a light boat, and, by means of muffled oars and under cover of the darkness, it is carried into the very midst of the sleeping ducks, and, being fired into their thick columns, great numbers are destroyed as well as crippled. This plan of killing wild fowl, however, is very generally reprobated by all respectable parties interested in this sport, and is very properly restricted by legislative enactment. Notwithstanding, however, the general discountenance of the community and the severe penalties threatening the participators in this cruel plan of butchery, many unprincipled poachers, who shoot for the markets, boldly resort to this expedient to fill their slender purses, in spite of all law and the universal execrations of those who live in the neighborhood of the bay. These impudent and reckless fellows know full well the inefficiency of all such laws, owing to the disinclination, or rather want of energy, on the part of the people to enforce them; for, without the assistance of those interested in such matters, all legislative enactments in reference to the preservation of game soon become obsolete, and the laws are no more than a dead letter.

"Strong efforts, however, were made at the last session of the Maryland legislature to do something towards the protection of the wild fowl on the Chesapeake, by the suppression of the surface-boats and the use of large guns; but the enactment was of little avail as regards the surface-boats, owing to some unlooked-for defect in the framing of the act, and we now learn that there is some probability of its being repealed altogether, which we very much regret: we would much rather see it made more rigid and then strictly enforced.

"Nothing is better calculated to drive ducks from their accustomed feeding-grounds than the practice of boating them at night; for, being disturbed during their wonted hours of repose and security by an unforeseen enemy, they soon learn that there is no safety for themselves under any circumstances, and have been known to abandon such places almost entirely after being shot at two or three times in the quiet of the night, when perhaps the whole flock, perfectly unconscious of danger, were wrapped in deep sleep.

"Boating ducks on their feeding-grounds, even with small guns during the daytime, will soon drive them from their accustomed haunts, and force them to find other spots at a distance where they can remain undisturbed. All modes of boating ducks are condemned by the sportsmen visiting these parts, as well as by those who reside in the vicinity of the bayshore.

Netting Ducks.

"A very ingenious way of taking canvas-backs was resorted to a few years since by a gentleman living on the bay, and which certainly, for its novelty, requires some notice on our part. This plan consisted in sinking gilling-nets a short distance below the surface of the water, so that the ducks in diving would get their heads and wings entangled in its meshes, and thus miserably perish by drowning.

"Great numbers were secured by this method at

first; but the canvas-backs soon entirely forsook the shoals where these nets were placed, and did not return to them again during the same season. But what brought this method more particularly into disrepute, even among pot-hunters, was the circumstance of the ducks secured in this way being so far inferior to those which were shot, owing to their being drowned and remaining so long a time under the water, as the placing of the nets occupied so much time and labor that it would not pay to examine them oftener than once in twenty-four or forty-eight hours; and many of the ducks, consequently, were under the water during a greater portion of this time. The flesh, under these disadvantages, became watery and insipid, and the ducks, moreover, were very hard to keep, except in excessively cold weather, on account of their bodies absorbing so much water. The whole system of gilling ducks is now entirely abandoned, and we only mention it as one of the things that have appeared and passed away. This method, however, of taking ducks is not altogether new, as a somewhat similar plan is resorted to on the coast of France for taking the scoter-duck, which little fowl resorts in considerable numbers to the sea-coast for the purpose of feeding on the shell-fish that there abound. The fishermen, or those engaged in taking wild fowl, spread their nets at low tide on the flats where these shell-fish are found, being supported two or more feet from the ground, so that the ducks, feeding in with the tide and diving after food, become entangled, as in the case of the canvas-backs, in the meshes of the net.

Dug-outs.

"Another very successful mode of killing ducks, and one which has been very much in vogue for many years on our rivers, is the use of the dig-outs or dug-outs,* a small kind of boat moored over the flats, and concealed as far as possible from observation by quantities of eel-grass thrown over it. Thus fixed, and surrounded by large numbers of decoys that are previously anchored all around the little vessel, the shooter patiently awaits the approach of the wild ducks which are flying up and down the river, and are, of course, tempted to dart down upon the deceptive decoys, believing them to be others of their own species that are feeding in perfect security, notwithstanding the proximity of the greenish mass which conceals the shooter and his boat. As soon as the canvas-backs have come sufficiently near, the shooter rises up suddenly and blazes away with his ponderous weapon, dealing death and destruction throughout the affrighted ranks of his unsuspecting victims.

"When the weather is favorable and the ducks are flying, this plan succeeds very well, and offers considerable attractions in the way of sport to those accustomed to wild-fowl shooting; but if the weather be cold and boisterous, none should attempt it but those inured to the roughest usage and who are perfectly regardless of the state of the elements.

* " So termed from being constructed by excavating the trunk of a large tree sufficiently deep to allow the person of the shooter to lie concealed in it."

Point Shooting.

"The really sportsmanlike way of killing canvas-backs is for the shooter to station himself on some one of the many *points* or *bars* along the bay-shore or its tributaries that the ducks fly over in their course to and from their feeding-grounds. Much depends, in this kind of shooting, upon the disposition of the elements; for neither pleasure nor success can be reasonably expected if the weather is intensely cold or the wind blowing fresh from a quarter that carries the ducks off from the point rather than on it.

"On the other hand, if the wind and weather prove favorable and the ducks are flying briskly, there is not a more delightful way of enjoying one's self than in point-shooting. Great skill and judgment are requisite to strike the ducks; and when thus suddenly stopped in their rapid course, they present a beautiful sight as they come tumbling down with a heavy plash from a height of one, two, or even three, hundred feet.

"It is this kind of duck-shooting that either displays the ignorance or dexterity of the sportsman; for, without long practice in this particular branch, the best general shooter in the country would appear to little advantage alongside even of an indifferent ducker."

Harbor Shooting.

In New England, all along the coast, we have what we call Harbor Shooting, and it forms a very desirable part of wild-fowl shooting. It is a kind of sport that cannot compare either in ease or results to duck shooting on the Chesapeake, yet it furnishes to many New England sportsmen a pleasure not to be derided.

The bleak rough coast of New England hardly furnishes an abiding place for any species of game, and the wild fowl that are found here come as visitors or sojourners. It is therefore the duty of the sportsman to be possessed of a knowledge of the times of arrival of the various kinds of fowl, and accordingly to have his house in order.

Shooting on the coast is called harbor shooting, and consists in taking a small keel boat, large enough to be safe, but light enough to row easily, and from ten to twenty wooden decoys of various kinds, for such ducks as are in season, and anchoring off some point of rocks which the fowl are accustomed to pass over, and then shooting them either as they fly past, or as they light among the decoys. The decoys should be attached to each other by a strong cord, and placed about twenty-five yards above the boat; that is, if the fowl are going south, as they generally are in the autumn, have the decoys north of the boat about that distance. If possible, have the boat anchored *bow on* towards the decoys. The tide and wind will not always allow this to be done. This position, however, should be maintained, if possible;

SHOOTING ON NEW ENGLAND COAST.

as, if the side of the boat be turned toward the decoys, it shows more surface for the fowl to see.

The sportsman should take with him in the boat two good double-barrelled duck guns (one of them a breech-loader, if possible); and have them ready loaded, lying on the thwart of the boat, with the hammers at half-cock for safety.

Coot Shooting.

When in position, the sportsman, sees a flight of coot at a distance coming towards him, he should drop quietly into his boat, and, bending his head down, peep up at the game from under the brim of his hat. As the coot come near the decoys, and are about to alight, the sportsman should wait until they begin flapping their wings preparatory to settling down. When he observes this motion, he should quickly give them both barrels of one of his guns, shooting at the lower parts of their bodies. Such a shot is recommended for the reason that the feathers and wings of the coot being open and extended, the charge has a chance to take greater effect than when the coot are in the water, with only their heads and part of their bodies out, and the latter snugly covered with their wings and feathers. Should the game not alight, and evince only an intention of swinging in toward the decoys for the purpose of taking a look at them, the sportsman should not fire until they are directly opposite. Then he should partly rise, and give them a quartering shot with both barrels; and if he has time, he should give them the contents of the other gun also. Be sure to put the gun well forward, and keep it moving even after it is discharged.

As a general rule, no man ever shoots too far forward of any wild fowl while on the wing.

If the coot are forty or fifty yards distant, and come down before a strong wind, it will not be too much to shoot ten or twelve feet in advance of them.

I would not recommend shooting the second gun after having discharged both barrels of the first, unless you have a sure chance. You will want the other barrels for the cripples, the securing of which will often require considerable finishing; otherwise they may disappear under water, and go away to leeward before showing themselves again. This sudden disappearance of the coot under the water is termed by the old wild-fowlers "putting on the pot-cover."

It is truly wonderful to see how long coot and some of the other wild fowl will remain under water, and the distance they will swim before coming to the surface. If not badly hurt when shot at, they will by turns dive quickly and come up again, showing their heads erect as they rise to the surface. In such a case it is useless to chase them with boat and gun.

It is always best to have a boatman along, to take the entire charge of the boat and decoys, and to do the pulling for the cripples, while the wild-fowler attends solely to the shooting. When in the boat, do all the shooting yourself, and you will not get shot through the carelessness of others.

In order to avoid shooting over the wounded coot

as they lie upon the water, bear down the sight of the gun close to the water, especially if the fowl are near to you. If they are at a long distance, make a little allowance for the declination of the shot by gravitation.

It is almost useless to shoot at the breast of any wild fowl when flying or swimming directly towards you, unless it is very close at hand. Their batting of feathers is pressed so closely to their bodies, by the pressure of the air or water, that it is hardly possible for shot to enter them. You may perhaps strike their heads or break their wings; but the more certain way has been already suggested.

In shooting at coot sitting on the water, always fire when they are rising on the wave, so that you can see their heads and necks. This will send the whole charge directly into their bodies. I have seen young sportsmen, who did not know or heed this rule, fire many times at a coot without hurting him. If possible, always shoot at their sides or tails.

Few waterfowl of the duck kind require so much punishing, or are able to bear so much hard shooting, as the coot. He is certainly a powerful fellow, whether we consider his power of flight or his faculty of remaining under water while swimming long distances, or the quickness with which he dives again if he sees any danger near at hand. The sportsman must be a good snap shot who, standing in readiness, can at the instant a coot sticks his head out of water give him a dead shot.

"Simple as a coot" is a common saying, and never

was there a more erroneous one, as any sportsman or wild-fowler will support me in saying. Those who, never having tried coot shooting, are disposed to doubt my statement and adhere to the old saw, will be likely to change their minds after a week's work in shooting at these birds from a boat.

BRANT SHOOTING. (*Anas birnicla.*)

THE time for shooting brant (or brent) along our New England coasts is in the spring, and the season for nearly all other kinds of wild fowl being in the autumn, brant shooting gives New England sportsmen about the only — we might safely say the only desirable — wild-fowl shooting at this season of the year.

Brant are well worth the attention and study of the sportsman, although he may never have occasion to pull trigger on one of them. Like all migratory birds and water-fowl, they have their appointed times for leaving the warm regions of the South for the colder climate of the North. They begin their flights about the middle of March, and in getting to their Northern breeding-grounds take considerable time, as they journey along in an easy manner, stopping frequently at good feeding-places on the way, particularly at various points on Chesapeake Bay and Long Island, until they reach Cape Cod. Here they usually stop for several days for the purpose of preparing for a more extended flight. They prune themselves on the sand-bars, and also fill their crops with sand; which last operation is called "taking in ballast." Having rested themselves, pruned their feathers into good order and taken in ballast, they rise from the bars in a spiral flight, called *towering up*, until they reach a great altitude, when they strike off in a direct line for Prince Edward Island, Labrador, and other stopping-places.

The manner of shooting brant usually adopted on Cape Cod, is this :—

Sportsmen at the beginning of the season build on the shore a sort of shanty large enough to accommodate some eight persons, in which they live while pursuing their avocation.

At some little distance from the hut, and near the water, as it rises at high tide, they dig out a hole in the sand large enough to set in, just below the surface, a good-sized wooden shooting-box capable of holding three shooters. At easy shooting distance from this box they build up a sand-bar with barrows and shovels a little higher than the level of the beach. On this bar the sportsmen place some live brant decoys securely fastened by cords.

When the tide comes in, the brant come in with it for the purpose of pruning themselves on the shore. The sand around this extemporized bar being covered with water by the rise of the tide, the bar itself is left above the water and presents an inviting place for the fowl to congregate, and the brant, seeing the decoys sitting safely upon it, eagerly swim to and mount alongside them. Then the three sportsmen in the box, seeing this happy state of things, shove out their double-barrelled shot-guns carefully, and shoot simultaneously by the given word, and each one toward the part of the bar agreed upon.

In this way they make sure destruction of their game, often killing from thirty to forty brant at one concerted shot.

Brant closely resemble the wild goose in color, habits, and general appearance; though they are much smaller, and might with some propriety be called the young wild goose. Indeed, Wilson classifies the brant as belonging to the goose species, and sportsmen often call it the brant goose. Brant make a hoarse, discordant sound, which once heard will be remembered. Their average weight is about four pounds. In my own mind they are as much associated with the wild goose as the quail is with the northern partridge. They are uncommonly wary. A piece of board or paper the size of a man's hand, a footprint on the sand, or the least unnatural appearance in the ground around them, will be seen by their eagle eyes, and will keep them from coming to the decoys.

There is work in this kind of sea shooting. The sand-bars usually have to be made over every day or two, and the shooting-boxes cleaned from the water that usually comes in at high tide. But with all these drawbacks, the hardy sportsman enjoys this hunting very much and is glad when the annual season for brant shooting returns.

RABBIT SHOOTING.

AMERICAN HARE. (*Lepus sylvaticus.*)

THIS is uncommonly good sport for the hunter, and much improves the shooting of the young sportsman, with respect to snap-shots. The sportsman does not indeed shoot on the wing, unless a partridge happen occasionally to start near him; but he shoots at a game which, when under full chase, with a pack of hounds close behind, will make the tyro think he never saw running before, especially if the hares be full-grown.

I once had a white hare pass near me, on a cross curving line, so swiftly that he appeared not to touch the snow at all, but seemed to go like a snowball thrown through the air. When on the transit, or directly opposite, it was impossible for me to get my gun on him, but I stopped him after he had passed, by giving him a quarter-shot. This fellow was clearing fourteen feet at each jump, by actual measurement, and he was closely pursued by the hounds who had just started him, and who were making the woods ring merrily in the early frosty morning.

How it stirs the blood as one hears in the distance the mellow sound of the hounds, when the hare is started! If you are close on his run and he happens to be coming towards you, leaping between the dark heavy pines and oaks, or dodging the bogs and stumps, as is usually the case, with his head thrown back and his eyes standing out from it, and resembling balls of fire, it will require the utmost steadiness of your nerves, and the instantaneous command of your wits, to get a shot at him. At such times look sharp, watch well your openings, and as soon as he comes within range, put your gun forward, according to the distance, as in shooting on the wing, and blaze away. At such times a sportsman should have no doubt or hesitation about when or how he should shoot. He has no time for either. He must act, I might almost say, instinctively as well as instantaneously; and should consider that, however disadvantageous the shot may appear to him, in all probability he will not get another or a better one at the same animal.

As hares and rabbits are hunted generally when there is a light fall of snow upon the ground, there is but little difficulty in finding their tracks when their haunts are known. In putting out the dog he should be made to follow the track in the direction of the game; and if the track be a fresh one, he will soon have the hare or rabbit up. If the track be one made the night previous, it may take the dog some little time to work it up.

Having placed your dog on the trail, your next thing is to get into position : that is, to take your stand at a point where the hare when started by the dog will run past you. To get a good or sure position requires judgment, and in selecting one, much depends upon the lay of the land. If it be low and swampy and surrounded by heavy timber, the hare will be very likely to run in the edge of the timber; particularly so if, on examination there, you find tracks made the night before. In all such places hares and rabbits usually have their regular runways, or paths, to which they take themselves whenever started ; and it is by examining these that the sportsman can best tell where to place himself. He will endeavor to get a position covering as many runways as possible. Dogs on taking a trail usually work it quietly until they come up with the hare or rabbit. Some, however, give occasional yelps ; but these are never mistaken for the general hullabaloo they make when they start their game. They then give tongue in quite a regular way, and a sportsman, knowing well the ground, and able to trace by his ear the course of the dog, can judge with much certainty the run and place of turning up of the game.

When the hare or rabbit has been started, and the sportsman has taken his position, he should stand perfectly still, with his eyes and ears wide open, whether he hears the dog or not ; for a hare oftentimes will take a dog off on a long chase, and then bring him back to the place, or near the place, he started from. After a hare has been started, he is likely to come upon you at any moment; and unless you are prepared to take him without the slightest hesitation the moment he shows himself, he will be gone.

I do not think it wise to run from one position to another unless you are very well acquainted with the ground; for both hares and rabbits have very sharp eyes, and will detect the slightest movement of your person. If they see nothing about you to frighten them, they will not hesitate to come very near you.

If well ahead of the dog, a hare will not always run at full speed. Occasionally he will stop, cock himself up on his hind-legs like a monkey, and work his big ears back and forth in the endeavor to hear the dog. He will frequently try to puzzle his pursuer, and will often succeed in doing so. I have known hares, when well ahead of the dogs, to go back on their tracks for some distance, and then jump off on one side with a long leap, so that when the hounds came to the end of the track, they were sorely puzzled. An experienced hound will not be thrown off the track easily by this skilful manœuvre. Dogs are up to this trick, and whenever they come to such an abrupt ending of the track, they at once go back on it, closely examining it for several feet on each side until they strike the fresh trail. In cases, however, where the hare back-tracks, the sportsman should assist his dog. He can generally tell when the dog has met with this little *contretemps*, by his not giving tongue. On approaching scrub-oaks or scattered cover, the hare, when followed, will sometimes stop and listen for the dog. Should he come up and stop within a short distance of you, do not think of taking advantage of him, but wait until he starts again before shooting. You will then give him some chance for his life, and will add much to your pleasure in finally killing him. Though I have had plenty of chances, I have never killed more than one or two hares or rabbits while sitting; and cannot recollect ever killing more than one in his nest — the circumstances then being such that I should have lost him if I had not done so.

After killing your hare or rabbit, let the dog come up and find him on the track where he was shot, as it satisfies and encourages the hound to ascertain that all is right.

Hares are usually found in large, heavy swamps of pine timber, or among the scrub-oaks adjoining such swamps; and they seldom take to hole, unless very hard pressed by the hounds. It is therefore much better sport to hunt the hare than the little gray rabbit, which will often hole soon after it is started. Rabbits also are found in scrub-oaks, and in low grounds among the alders, in good location for woodcock. They are not often found in the middle of heavy pine-timbered swamps, but occasionally on the edges. They are very rapid in their movements, giving a quick turn, and soon get out of sight, but they do not run so far before stopping as the hare. They both *lie in their nests*, as it is called, alike; often under the lower limbs of a pine tree, standing up close to the body, or in the swamp, where a low bush makes a temporary cover. It is strange that they do not freeze. I have often wondered how the little conies manage to live during the extreme cold weather of winter, as their nests or covers are but the slightest protection to them; yet they are never found frozen. They live in the winter by browsing upon the ends of certain bushes and limbs, and by eating the bark of trees, — the black birch is their particular favorite; and on this simple food they keep themselves fat and sleek in spite of all their exposure.

Hares and rabbits in leaping bring their hind feet forward and outside of their fore-legs. This peculiar mode of progression causes them to curve up their backs, and at the same time gives them great power to spring. It gives also to their leaping a peculiar motion, something like the movement of a rocking-horse, or of a deer when running, — a rolling, half-circular motion. In examining the tracks of a hare or a rabbit, it is therefore worthy of note that the forward prints are made with the hind feet. In shooting this game, it is better not to take them either at the height of their jump or when close to the ground, but between the two extremes.

The hound never catches the hare or rabbit; at least I never knew one to do it; and it would be a wonder if he did, in the kind of hunting of which I am speaking. Rabbit hounds go entirely by scent, and do not see far ahead in following the tracks. I have several times shot rabbits so near to the head of the hounds that they, not always following the exact line of the track, have gone past and some distance beyond its termination, without knowing where the rabbits were, until the loss of the fresh scent stopped them. The rabbit will easily dodge the hound in the chase. The greyhound is the best dog for this kind of sport, and the open prairie is the best place for it. Even there the short and sudden turns of the rabbit are likely to be too much for the hound, who, although a rapid runner, and leaping twice as far as the rabbit, and going entirely by sight, yet is so apt to go past and over the rabbit, in every imaginable way, that the latter, taking advantage of all the favorable points of the ground, will usually contrive to escape.

A singular circumstance once happened while I was shooting hares and rabbits in the winter alone. I was in a thick, dark swamp some five or six miles in extent, and an excellent place for both kinds of game — hares and rabbits. The swamp rejoiced in the appellation of the "Devil's Den"; so called because it was supposed that no one, except the Old Fellow himself, could get through some of the thickest and miriest parts of it. Having killed several white hares (for it was in December), I was just passing into the more open part of the "Den," near some alders, when I discovered a gray rabbit sitting at the foot of a large pine tree. My dog being away in search of game, I walked boldly up, until within easy killing distance; but I despised the idea of shooting him while sitting. I concluded he would cross the open space to the alders on my left, which he did; and when on the jump, I gave him a charge, at which he stopped immediately, with his head cocked up, apparently wondering what was the matter. My first thought was to give him the other barrel; but applying my rabbit-rule of "no running, no shooting," I walked straight up to him, put my hand upon him, and found him — stone dead! At his last jump, the snow, which was rather deep, had crowded around him in such a way as to hold up his head, making him look very life-like. This was the first and only rabbit that I ever "killed a-standing," and it was certainly the first and last time that I ever knew one to " stand a killing."

Rabbits are not Hares, and Hares are not Rabbits.

Hares are much larger and heavier than rabbits, apparently about twice as large. Hares have extremely long hind legs, and are very rapid runners. Probably nothing is harder to shoot than one of either of these animals as they spring from their nests. It is astonishing how soon they disappear. Often, with a mere flurry like the movement of a partridge, they are gone, you cannot tell where. At such times, I think a hare or rabbit is more difficult to kill than any bird that flies.

In this country the hare begins to turn white in November, when he is sprinkled with gray. About the middle of December, when the snow comes, his hair is a pure white; and but few animals which the sportsman drops with his gun are handsomer. His fur begins to turn gray again in March; and in the summer months it is entirely of a gray color.

The fur of the white rabbit is used for muffs and other furrier work; their skin is very tender, but when tanned in alum twenty-four hours can be handled easily, and is quite strong. As long as hares are so cheap in the market, their furs will not be sought for. The watchmakers and jewellers used formerly to purchase their hind legs and use the foot pad to polish silver with, the fur being very soft and thick.

It is remarkable how they will slip past the hunter in the new snow, spreading their feet and legs to cover as much surface as possible. They will often pass the young sportsman, and within a short distance of him, without his knowing it.

Respecting the qualities of the hare for the table, all I can say is, some people are fond of them. I am not; they are too *gamey* for my taste.

Not so, however, with the rabbit. Nothing is nicer than the fore saddle of a good fat gray October rabbit. In fact all parts are good. Parboil him, and then stew him up like a fricasseed chicken, with plenty of good butter and salt pork, and you will have a dish " equalled by few, and excelled by none."

THE SETTER AND POINTER.

A NEW WAY OF TRAINING THEM.

MY experience in dog-training is not extensive; for although I always loved a well-trained bird-dog, I never fancied the work of training one. I believe, nevertheless, that in order to secure the best and most trustworthy work in the field, the hunter should train his own dog.

The *modus operandi* I would suggest is as follows: Take a young dog of good breed, setter or pointer (I prefer the former), when about six months old. Have him kept in a safe place, where no one will handle or feed him but yourself, and feed him by hand as far as possible. A warm shed, wagon-house or barn is a good place: these dogs are always fond of a horse.

The first lesson with the dog should be to teach him obedience, and to "down" at the word. Some use the word "charge"; I dislike it. It is not a natural word; neither is it so easily spoken, nor so full in sound, as the other. Afterwards I should begin with a medium-sized, leather-covered ball — such as the dog can easily manage, throwing it and teaching him to bring it and drop it on the ground or in the hand, and making him "down" at the same time. This part of the training is usually only half done. It should be repeated every day until the dog is thoroughly familiar with his lesson.

Make the dog keep his distance and his place in all his trainings. Don't let him jump on you, and do not fool with him; if you do, your teaching will be in a great measure lost. Always treat him evenly and kindly, and he will soon know what you mean. Many people, and especially boys, spoil good hunting dogs that are naturally excellent ones, by kicking them at one moment, and caressing them at another, until the poor creatures do not know what to expect or what to do under any circumstances.

Then a dog should have but one master, and the master should keep his temper while training, bearing in mind that he himself has been twenty-one years in learning to be a man.

After the dog retrieves well, and will drop the ball to your feet or hand, and will *down* at the word, take your gun, and after letting him see it and smell it, snap a few caps before him so that he may become used to the sound. There is much risk of frightening a dog at this point, and to such an extent as to render him useless. I have known dogs with excellent points irreparably injured at this stage of their training, by having a gun suddenly fired at or near them. I would therefore recommend that the caps be snapped as the ball is thrown for the dog to bring in, as he will then not notice it so much. This should be done quite often, until he gets acquainted with the gun; when he has become accustomed to it, — and it will not take him long to do so, — he will, whenever he sees his master handling it, expect a good time at playing ball.

The next step should be to take the dog and gun into a field and find a robin, or a chipping-bird, which shoot with a light charge of powder and shot, and make the dog bring to you if you can. If he will not readily do it, take the dead bird and perform as with the ball, and if he will retrieve and give to hand, and *down*, he is getting along very well.

In shooting the birds keep the dog down by your side, and in order to accustom him to the gun let him frequently smell the muzzle of it.

If he manifests no great fear of the gun when fired, and will retrieve as above suggested, roam about with him in the fields, killing occasionally any bird you may come across. Pointers and setters both like sporting about, and a short experience of this sort will soon accustom them to the gun; and instinctively they will associate its appearance in the hands of their master with their own freedom and sport.

Take home your dead birds with you, lay aside your gun, and begin throwing your ball again and let the dog bring it as before; then throw out your dead birds one at a time, and he will be pretty sure to bring them to you. Now put up the dog in his kennel, and let him rest. Go out alone and shoot a robin if near by, or a tame pigeon. Bring it in as soon as you can, and while it is warm hide it under some hay or old grass, in the same direction in which you have always played with the ball. Now take out the dog again, and let him bring in the ball once or twice. Then roll it so as to leave it as near the dead bird as you can, and you will notice that, when he goes for the ball, he will surely come to a point on the dead bird, if he has a good nose. Should he make a point, let him make a good long stand, and then shoot your gun with a light charge, telling him to bring. Should he retrieve well, and drop the bird to hand and *down* at the command, you need not fear his proving other than a good hunter. All you may require of him will come by practice.

I would observe that I trained my best setter with the ball and fresh-killed bird.

I did not, however, go into the field, as here recommended, but broke him entirely with the ball, finishing off with the dead bird, as above described. This system of training I may say is entirely original with me. I had never seen it practised, or heard of it, before I trained my dog; and speaking from the result, as shown by my own dog, I can state that it has proved entirely successful.

It was but a short time after I had trained my dog in this way that I had an opportunity to test him. Passing through a field late one afternoon in December, when snow was on the ground, I accidentally flushed a covey of quail. I went immediately home, got my gun and dog, and started out after them.

That afternoon and the next morning I shot and bagged twelve out of the covey of fourteen; and never has my dog worked better than he did then.

The only thing to be guarded against, in this method of training, is the disposition of the dog to chase the bird when he puts him up. I think quail are the best game-birds to train the dog with, as they are usually found in open fields and hedges, and you can attend to the working of the dog better than in covert-shooting. Should the dog be inclined to break for the bird after it is flushed, you can go forward and flush the bird yourself; or go round ahead of the bird, facing the dog, and then let him put up the bird. In either case command the dog to *down*, then shoot, and he will be likely to stop. If you find much trouble in making your dog obey, take a good shot into the field with you, and when the dog points you can attend to him, while your friend sees to the bird. You can then see that the dog *downs* as soon as he has flushed the bird.

This is the sum and substance of training the setter or pointer; and all that remains for the sportsman is to make his dog perfectly obedient. This is one of the greatest difficulties in the whole management of the bird-dog. If not brought under strict obedience, he will be apt, when in the cover, to take the trail of some game-bird and lead off out of sight and beyond the sound of the bell. Then it happens, as the sportsman often finds to his cost, that he must hunt his dog, instead of having his dog hunt for him, and be his servant. Work the dog with a bell, though not a loud one, as it will tend to make him deaf. Do not keep it on him except when he is working in the covert.

Do not feed your bird-dog with much meat during the summer months: at this season he requires but little, if any. For my dog I boil up a quantity of Indian pudding, feeding it out cold with a little milk, and at times adding some pot-liquor from boiled beef. During the hot days in summer, if your dog is housed in a kennel, knock out the bottom and let him have his bed on the bare ground; and now and then have the inside cleaned and whitewashed. Occasionally move the kennel along on the ground and give him a clean new bed; indeed, always have his bed clean, as it will tend to keep him cool and comfortable.

What my Setter did, trained in this Way.

One season, when woodcock were very scarce, I one day took a friend out hunting who had a great desire to see my setter work, particularly as he had had a number of dogs who were unsuccessful in their pointing.

It was a dry season, and we went by a mountainous route where I always hunted at such times. We passed through some excellent woodcock grounds, without flushing a feather. Coming at last to a little copse of woods and alders in an open pasture, I followed the dog into the covert, while my friend took the outside.

Soon after getting well into the cover, Dash came to a point on a woodcock. I gave him the word

"Steady," and backed round for a better position. While doing so I struck my boot against a little pine staddle, and just then up went an old partridge. I dropped her near the dog, and he, turning his head, and seeing the partridge lying on the ground flapping a wing, left his point, and went and brought her in. I reloaded as quickly as possible, and at the same time sent the dog back to his point. This he took handsomely, and at the word "Go," put the woodcock up; I dropped her also. I then sent the dog for the dead cock. On his way he came to another point, and, at the word, flushed another cock, which was likewise killed; the dog then brought in both birds, and gave them to hand.

Meeting my friend at the lower end of the covert, I told him I had started two woodcock and one partridge, and asked him if he had seen anything of them; looking at my bag with a cunning smile, he replied that he had not seen them, but he could guess where they were.

SHOOTING-DRESS.

MANY readers will perhaps think it foolish to mention such small matters as will come under this topic; but I can assure the young sportsman that all these little items materially increase or diminish the comfort of the hunter while in the field. Any old hunter will tell you that, by reason of some defect in his dress, such as a pair of ill-fitting boots, he has sometimes lost the pleasure of what would otherwise have been an excellent day's shooting. While I do not intend to define all the *minutiæ* of dress and equipments, — knowing that most hunters who live in the country put on their old clothes, as they should do, — still I hope the suggestions I have to make will not be without value, particularly to young sportsmen.

The shooting-jacket or coat should be about the size of a sailor's monkey-jacket, with one row of buttons in front, and not lapped, so that on a warm day it can be opened in front. It should be made of light-weight flannel, and as near the predominating color of the woods as possible. Let there be a large pocket on each side, and a small pocket on the right, half-way down, for the caps, which should be kept loose. There should also be a pocket for a handkerchief in the usual place, high up on the left. Pockets are handy, but I don't recommend too many of them, for the hunter when in haste is apt to get confused with them. Wear a vest of medium warmth, which can be opened when needed. I would always, when on shooting-ground, keep the upper button of the coat fastened, as otherwise it prevents the gun from coming to its place at the shoulder quickly; and in snap shooting you would be apt to lose your bird from this cause. For pants, have thin ones, if possible such as will ward off the briers. In summer and early fall shooting, heavy pants tire the sportsman much. I generally tuck mine into my boot-tops. For boots, good heavy calf-skin, or what are known as grained-leather boots, are good for use in the field, and turn water well. Do not have the boots too heavy; a pound or two extra on a pair of boots tells wonderfully in a long day's hunt. Have the whole boot strong and substantial as well as light. A light sole of leather, with a very light sole of rubber outside, makes a durable, dry, and easy boot; have the boots made straight, that is, not rights and lefts, and change them each time you hunt. Have the heels of the boots low and wide, with the soles wide, and not too thick. Let them fit as loosely as possible, without letting the heels slide up and down. Wear woollen stockings, if you can, even in summer. Woollen stockings prevent chafing on the sides of the foot and ankle. If your foot is inclined to chafe, rub the parts with oil before leaving home in the morning. Perhaps there is no part of the dress liable to give so much discomfort as the boot.

Some sportsmen wear laced-up shoes. They are

very fine, I admit, when the hunting-ground is always in the open field, and free from mud and water; and they are much used on the other side of the Atlantic. But I would not use them here, especially while hunting in low ground. Keep the boots well cleaned and greased. If the sportsman has much shooting to do, I would advise him to get two pairs of boots, so as to have one pair in order all the time. Do not have your boot-tops very high, unless you are going to hunt among briers. The young sportsman may think they look well coming up over the knee, like the cavalry boot; but in hot weather they heat the knee-joint, which should be kept cool.

For a shooting-hat or cap, I use, in-July, a medium-brim Panama or summer hat. I eschew caps at this season, notwithstanding they may look better and appear more jaunty; for they heat the head, which it is important to keep as cool as possible. In late fall shooting, a cap with a visor, or a soft hat with a medium brim, is the best.

I would simply add that, as the weather grows cool in the fall, it is better to wear the same coat then as during the warmer season, adding, however, a warmer vest.

Game-Bags.

Some people make game-bags of the pocket or lining of their hunting-coat, having the pockets lined with rubber cloth or other material. This is not my practice; there are many objections to this kind of bag. Whatever we might imagine to the contrary, it is a fact that the game is not nearly so easily carried in the large pocket of the coat. The July birds will not keep half so long, if carried in this manner. And when resting, the load cannot easily be thrown off the shoulder for the relief of the hunter. Moreover, should he be invited to dine at some good farmer's, and wish to appear as respectable as possible for a Nimrod, the young ladies might not admire the peculiar odor coming from the shooting-jacket; and although he may have taken pains to remove all the game, the blood-stains will remain, and will look altogether too unbecoming and filthy for any respectable sportsman.

In selecting a bag, get a wide, thick strap for the shoulder, and it will not hurt you, while a thin one, of sheep-skin or webbing, will wear your shoulder badly in a couple of hours, if you have a fair bag of game. There can be no compromise in this. Have an inside pocket in your game-bag divided into compartments for your luncheon, powder-flask, and shot-pouch. Even should you never use the flask or pouch from the bag, it is very convenient in keeping the packages together in travelling or moving about, or while it is hanging in your room, as it saves multiplicity of pieces. If you have a bag made by some shoemaker, (which is the better way,) have your net made like corded shad-nets, which have been tanned to prevent their decay; they will then be strong, and will not easily break in the covert. Do away with all toggery about your bag, remembering that a fancy border hanging down is a mere nuisance when you are in the covert, and that all gaudy trimming is detestable to an experienced hunter. Let the bag be of good width, and always have the part next the body of heavy calf-skin or sheep-skin; the former is far preferable. A thin bag of cloth or rubber cloth, will soon make your hip and side sore by the friction, which a medium thick calf-skin will never do. I would not take one of the thin bags as a gift.

Powder-Flasks and Shot-Pouches.

It is hardly necessary to say much with reference to these articles, although they form an important part of every sportsman's equipments. It is not at all difficult to select a good flask or pouch, as there are so many good ones in the market. I will merely state that the Waterbury Flask and Cap Company of Connecticut make a style of flask that I like very much, particularly those which are covered with leather, and have German silver tops. Dixon's English flasks are also good, but they cost much more than the American ones. The Waterbury flasks, or some of them, have in one respect a superiority over all other flasks I am acquainted with. The hole opening into the charger is of the proper size, — of sufficient dimensions to admit of rapid filling. It is not very pleasant, in loading with haste, to have to snap your flask two or three times before getting your charge of powder down. In duck-shooting particularly, I have used the Waterbury "quick-loaders," as they are called, with more satisfaction than any other flasks I ever handled.

For shot-pouches I would recommend those made by the Waterbury Company, or by Dixon, the English manufacturer.

Gun-Wads and Caps.

It is universally acknowledged that Eley's caps are the best, and indeed about the only ones fit for use. Always get those that fit tightly, without splitting when the hammer is down : the best are the cheapest.

For gun-wads I also use Eley's. Get those that are one size larger than the gauge. If the gauge is 14, get 13 wads; though, as a cover for the shot, they are rather thick and heavy, and add to the kick of the gun. I sometimes have two kinds in each pocket of my shooting-dress, — a thick wad and a thin one,— the latter being intended for the cover of shot. When the gun is foul, it is hard to drive down a heavy wad; nor does the shot require it.

If you live in the country, where you cannot purchase cut wads, make your own. Get from the shoemaker's a quantity of waste scrap leather, and let it be thick and somewhat spongy. With your wad-cutter (every owner of a gun should keep one) cut out your wads on the end of a log of wood, recollecting to make them one size larger than the bore of the gun. With judgment in the selection of your leather, you can thus get an excellent wad at little expense. For several seasons I have used this kind exclusively, and I consider them much better than those which are cut from pasteboard.

Shot-Cartridges.

I have for years been wishing that some experienced person would invent a shot-cartridge that would overcome many of the objections to, or difficulties encountered in, using loose shot. Eley's cartridges have, to a certain extent, been a step in the right direction ; but they fail to answer what is required, and are not generally used by our best sportsmen. They serve to show, however, the fact that shot fired in a loose form from the gun are propelled, as regards force and concentration, at a great loss of effect from what would be the result could they be encased in a cartridge compact in form, that would open at the proper distance. Shot scatter widely when fired from the gun in the usual manner, for the very obvious reason that each shot receives its propellent force at an angle to its line of direction. The pellets of shot being round, and the force of the discharge pressing one pellet against the other, the shot in the lower layers are crowded as much as possible into the interstices of those above them, and, pushing the pellets of the upper layers out of their position, cause them to take very divergent directions when expelled from the muzzle of the gun. As the shot lie in numerous layers in the barrel, the whole force of the combustion of the powder is received by the lower layer, which communicates its impetus to the layer above, and this one to the next in turn, and so on.

The lower layers, having spent much of the impetus given them in pushing the upper layers along, when they reach the muzzle, are weakened in their force, and do not continue so far as the upper layers. It will be seen, therefore, that a charge of shot exhausts upon itself a good portion of the force given it by the powder, and consequently that portion of the charge which does become effective receives the least direct force from the powder.

I am not without hope but that, with the increasing taste for sporting, and also on account of the scientific knowledge brought to bear upon the manufacture of all things appertaining to the gun, we shall ultimately have a cartridge that will answer all practical demands. Such a cartridge is needed; and if one could be made at a reasonable price, one that would not ball, but open at the required distance, it would meet with universal favor.

RECOIL.

THE subject of recoil, I do not think, is generally understood. Almost every one knows when a gun kicks, and some of the causes of its kicking; but all do not fully understand why one gun kicks more than another, or the laws by which the phenomenon is governed.

Action and reaction being equal and in opposite directions, it follows that the recoil of a musket or fowling-piece is in proportion to the quantity of powder used, the weight of the gun, and the obstruction in the passage. All guns recoil more or less, from the amount of powder used in their discharge. But what the sportsman should particularly attend to are the causes which produce excessive recoil, or kicking, and which, in the case of guns of the same calibre and weight, loaded with equal charges of powder and shot, make one kick more violently than another. This question of recoil underlies all the essential differences found between guns. Two persons may have guns made by the same maker, exactly alike in length, weight, bore, and quality of iron, of which one will shoot well up to the mark, while the other behaves but indifferently; and the difference in the recoil will perhaps be considerable. This is because, in one of the guns, there is some slight inequality of the bore, some retraction or unevenness, however small, which throws back the gases while the powder is burning, and thus makes the gun kick, instead of discharging evenly and without extra friction, as in a perfect cylinder. Any slight substance adhering to the inside of the barrel, or the fact that one part of the barrel is thicker than another, diminishing the evenness and elasticity, may operate in a similar way. With all the care taken by barrel-makers, in the manufacture of the choicest and highest-priced guns, they well know how difficult it is to get them of true and even proportions and weight.

Again, barrel-makers find serious difficulty in making the tube perfectly straight and true inside. Although their accurate and accustomed eyes can usually tell if there is much inequality, they often find, by introducing a close-fitting iron plug with a piston-rod attached, that there is an obstruction in some part of the passage. Any obstruction or inequality, however slight, hinders the free discharge of the shot or bullet from the gun, and causes proportionately just so much recoil, detracting from the force of the shot and the evenness of the shooting.

Foulness is one chief cause of the excessive kicking of many guns; and this can be easily accounted for, since the barrels become lined with dirt from the many discharges of the gun, as all experienced sportsmen know. It is especially to be noticed in duck-shooting. After some twenty shots have been fired from one barrel, with equal quantities of powder, the gun recoils much more violently than at first. On this account many sportsmen reduce the charge of powder when the guns have become quite foul. If very foul, not only will the gun recoil badly, but, if it be a light one, the barrels are apt to become strained by the explosion.

The increase or decrease of recoil is to a considerable extent governed by the position in which the gun is held. If it be discharged vertically, (which should never be done, lest a broken shoulder be the consequence,) the recoil is increased some fifty per cent by the gravitative force of the earth. If discharged perpendicularly, the recoil is diminished in the same proportion in which it is increased by the vertical discharge. These facts should be remembered by the sportsman.

The more firmly the gun is held to the shoulder when fired, the less will the recoil be felt; not that the recoil is less in itself, but the pressure upon the body lessens the sensation. The sportsman can also shoot to a greater distance by holding the gun close to the shoulder. The recoil is apt to be much weaker in shooting on the wing, or at any moving object, than in shooting at a target; for the excitement attendant upon shooting on the wing overcomes to a certain degree the feeling of the kick of the gun, although the recoil is the same, *minus* the velocity with which the gun is moved in following the bird, as in shooting at the target.

It is well known by ordnance men, in the army and navy, that cannon mounted on wheels have a great recoil, which lessens the force of the ball or other projectile. The French navy once adopted a spring cushion to receive the force of the recoil on board ships of war, in order to prevent the rolling of the vessel when in action. But they were obliged to discard it, because they thus lost in the discharge a force proportionate to that of the recoil.

The recoil of a shot-gun, loaded with a ball of the same weight, is much less than when loaded with shot. . The reason is, that the ball, being a compact body, starts easily, and moves through the barrel with much less friction than shot. The friction of the ball is on the extreme arc of the circle, or circumference; while the shot cover much more surface in the barrel, and, being loose, are somewhat wedged in their passage out.

It is on this account that I anticipate the invention of a cartridge for shot that will produce less friction in its passage through the barrel than now occurs, when the shot are fired in a loose state.

The amount of friction in different guns is so various, and the making often so imperfect, that it is impossible to estimate the recoil, except by a spring or something of the sort. In the ordinary gun for brush shooting, the recoil is probably not far from forty-five pounds. The shoulder is so strong and the pressure so evenly diffused over the body, that this may appear to be overstated. But I am inclined to think that the recoil will usually exceed rather than fall short of the figure I have mentioned.

Some have thought that the recoil of a fowling-piece depends much upon the manner in which the gunpowder is ignited from the fulminating powder of the cap, i. e. whether at the extreme base of the charge, or from the top or centre, or from the forward part of it. But from what I can learn from the experience of others who have tested the question, I think the point of ignition makes no material difference as to the recoil. I learn from a celebrated rifle-maker of this country that he has experimented without finding any perceptible difference. In this connection I will give, from the "Essay on Shooting," the statement of M. Le Clerc, gunsmith to the king of France in 1780, who was well informed on all subjects relating to his profession.

"These experiments," says M. Le Clerc, "were made with a barrel (flint lock) nearly thirty-two inches in length (English measurement), and weighed, with the loaded plank upon which it was fixed, twenty-eight pounds. The barrel had four touchholes, which could be stopped with screws. The charge consisted of one drachm and twelve grains of powder, from a royal manufactory, and eight drachms eighteen grains of shot, called small 4. The barrel was fired from each touchhole at a sheet of paper, measuring twenty by sixteen inches (French measure), placed at a distance of nearly forty-five ordinary paces." The only difference in loading was that, in the first set of experiments, the wads consisted of hat-felt, cut to fit the calibre, while in the latter paper wadding was used. Had these trials been made with no other motive than to determine the degree of recoil produced by the situation of the touchhole, there would have been no use in marking the size of the shot, the distance and dimensions of the mark, and the number of grains thrown into it at each discharge. From the experiment it appears, to use the words of M. Le Clerc, that, "with regard to the recoil, the distance of the touchhole from the breech is of little importance." The table accompanying the remarks quoted, giving the result of the various discharges, throughout the trial, shows that the mere point of ignition was immaterial.

If it were possible, when discharging the gun, to jerk it back with sufficient force, and at the right instant, the shot would drop harmless from the muzzle. Consequently, the sportsman who holds the gun most firmly to his shoulder will be able to kill at the greatest distance, other things being equal. Base-ball catchers have learned this secret, or they would have more broken fingers than they can now boast of. By dropping the hand, and gradually checking, so far as possible, the force of the heavily loaded ball, they avoid much of the punishment that would otherwise follow.

SCIENTIFIC MATTERS.

THE object of these remarks is to lead the intelligent sportsman to think for himself, devise plans of his own, and make such trials as may grow out of the study of the gun and its discharge. The gun, in all its separate and combined functions, is the result of much more scientific study than is usually supposed; embracing, as it does, the laws of strength, projectile force, elasticity, contractile force, and combustion. All this makes it a more complicated machine than almost any other engine of the same size. At the present time it demands all the scientific knowledge which the sportsman may possess, to fully understand its various parts, and to bring its execution up to the highest possible standard.

The question is often asked, Why is the chamber at the lower end of the barrel, running into the breech-pin, made in a concave or conical shape? One reason is, that this form helps to prevent what is called the *burning of the breech-pin.* When the old-fashioned square and even-surfaced pin was used, before the *patent chamber* was invented, we often heard the remark, as an excuse for a gun which did not shoot up to the mark, that "it must be breech-burnt." At present, with our patent chambers, we are not much troubled in this way; and my opinion is that, in former times, *rust* had more to do with the "burning of the breeches." than the powder ever had.

The next point to be considered in connection with the patent chamber is the addition to the force of the powder when discharged, and the partial diminution of the recoil. The additional force given to the discharge by powder, when burned in a conical breech, arises from the concentration and reaction of the gases in the cone at the extremity of the chamber. The extent of the reactionary force is considerable, acting as it does upon the outward pressure of the gases. Suppose a jet of water to enter a glass tumbler or tube, having a round or conical-shaped bottom, instead of a square or straight one, as is usually the case. The reaction of the water would be greatly increased by the conical shape of the base. So it is with the gases in the patent-chambered gun. The same principle may be noticed in the lanterns used on the front of railroad engines in the night. The reflectors having conical shapes, they throw the reflected light forward with great intensity. In fact, the reflection is stronger than the light itself. The recoil of the gun, moreover, is lessened by the lateral pressure of the gases along the sides of the chamber, while the reaction of the gases at the extreme point counteracts, to a certain extent, the force of the recoil. In fact, it is now generally admitted that in the patent-chambered guns the recoil is less than in the old-fashioned ones with a straight breech-pin, and that the force of the charge is increased.

In this connection I will add the results of some

scientific experiments made with the rifle, showing that, up to a certain point, the velocity of the bullet increases with its distance from the rifle. They are to be found in Greener's work on "The Science of Gunnery."

"In the report of the experiments which were carried on at Cork in 1852, it is stated that the power of penetration of an elongated rifle bullet gradually increases as the range is increased, up to 190 yards. In order to prove this, experiments were carried on at Enfield for three days, with a variety of fire-arms and different sorts of projectiles. On the fourth day, the experiments were repeated with the common musket and Wilkinson's rifle. The former at 40 yards gave a penetration of 2.25 inches; and the latter averaged 2.75 in a target of green elm. Again, at 90 yards, the musket penetrated 2.25 inches, and the rifle 3.5 inches. At 120 yards, the musket gave 2.5 inches, and the rifle 3.25. Both being subsequently fired at every successive ten yards up to 220, the result was that the penetration of the musket ball gradually decreased in power as the distance increased, while the elongated bullet gained power of penetration up to 190 yards; after which it slightly decreased.

"Consequent on the velocity of the explosive fluids is the resistance of that aeriform fluid filling all space. It has been calculated that, in a vacuum, matter in motion would be a long time in coming to rest; and very providential it is that Nature, in her grand arrangements, has made one element to control another.

"In no other portion of Nature's work has anything

more wonderful than atmospheric air been produced. Its action on the velocity of projectiles is of so extensive a nature that, without clearly understanding that action, the science of gunnery never can be thoroughly acquired. The resistance of the atmosphere is in proportion to the velocity of the attempt to displace it; the higher that velocity becomes, the greater the resistance."

There are many things in nature and science that act contrary to our preconcived ideas, as in the case of the bullet increasing its velocity after leaving the gun, up to 190 yards. It would be easy to extend this subject, and fill many more pages with analogous experiments. But I will not weary the reader with a multiplicity of them, and will give only one more well-known fact connected with the gun, showing the law of force, and the resistance of the air.

Take an old-fashioned American cent and fasten it against a heavy plank or wall, and no shot-gun ever made has sufficient force to drive shot through it in that position; but hang the cent in the air by a string at the distance of eight or ten paces from the muzzle of a gun loaded with a large charge of powder, say five or six drachms, and one layer of large shot, and the latter can be driven fairly through the cent, making holes in it like those in a pepper-box. It was also observed, during our recent war, that the plating of our iron-clads, no matter how thick, could be easily broken or pierced by the balls from the rifle-guns, while much thinner iron abutted on wood resisted them.

Combustion, to be available, must not be instantaneous. Time must be given for movement. Fulminating powder is, like lightning, more instantaneous in its effect than gunpowder. It does not act, however, as a propellent force, as its combustion is so instantaneous that no time is given for its environment to expand. A gun charged with fulminating powder would be apt to burst when ignited, on account of the charge not moving quick enough to accommodate the combustion.

The same thing is true, to some extent, with very fine-grained gunpowder, the combustion of which is much more instantaneous than powder of a coarser grain. Placed in a long-barrelled gun, it loses the accelerating power produced by slow combustion, and consequently its propellent force is greatly reduced, while the recoil is increased.

Greener quotes from a writer, who says : " If a train of gunpowder be crossed at right angles by a train of fulminating mercury, laid on a sheet of paper on a table, and the gunpowder lighted by a red-hot wire, the flame will run on until it meets the cross train of fulminating mercury, when the inflammation of the latter will be so instantaneous as to cut off the connection with the continuous train of gunpowder, leaving one half of the train unignited." And again : " If the fulminating powder be lighted first, it will go straight on, and pass through the train of gunpowder so rapidly as not to inflame it at all."

The explosive force of gunpowder, its pressure by the force of the gases, and the general law of com-

SCIENTIFIC MATTERS. 197

bustion, are questions that demand careful study to be understood; and the sportsman will not find his time misapplied who examines them carefully in detail.

The question as to whether or not the force of the charge is at all increased beyond the force of the immediate explosion at the breech-end of the gun, is one on which there are a variety of opinions. My own conviction, formed after much thought on the subject, is that the chief force of a given charge of powder is made within three or four inches from the breech or chamber of the barrels. As the charge proceeds out of the barrel, the gases expand, finding more room as the wad above the powder reaches the muzzle of the gun, and consequently on the passage the propellent force is somewhat diminished. It cannot possibly be increased if the combustion is complete at the breech end of the gun, as there is nothing more to make it an accelerating power. And this suggestion does not conflict with the statement that coarse powder being slower in its combustion than fine, its propellent gases are continued farther up the barrel, and give greater force to the charge.

If we estimate the force of two and one half drachms of gunpowder as equal to five thousand pounds, and then suppose this quantity to be instantly ignited at the chamber of the gun or a very few inches from it, then the whole force being instantly expended, it cannot in any conceivable way be increased in the barrel, between the place of ignition and its muzzle. Therefore. I think, so far as force alone is concerned, that short-barrelled guns (of the same bore) will throw their shot with as much power as longer ones that have the atmospheric pressure to meet, with the extra friction of the charge along the barrel, in its passage out.

I am also of the opinion that a small-bored gun with a medium charge of gunpowder, and a quantity of shot suited to it, will throw its shot to a greater distance than a larger bored gun *with the same quantity of powder;* and for this reason, that the powder in the smaller-bored gun lies higher up in the barrel, and consequently consumes more time in the burning. This conclusion favors, to some extent, the small-bored gun against the larger bore; but this favor, if allowed, can be carried only to a certain extent, as the tremendous recoil in the small-bored gun would prevent its use with a large increase in the quantity of powder.

GUNPOWDER.

THE discovery of gunpowder is generally conceded to have been made by a German monk, named Schwartz, about A. D. 1320; although the credit of this wonderful discovery has been claimed for others, among them Roger Bacon, born in 1214, who was the greatest physical philosopher of the Middle Ages, and well versed in such chemical science as then existed. At any rate, this discovery, like that of the art of glass-making and many others equally important, was purely accidental.

Gunpowder consists usually of about 75 parts of saltpetre or nitre, with 13 of charcoal, and 12 of sulphur. Different nations make a slight difference in the division of these elements. In very warm countries, more sulphur is used, to check the waste occasioned by the humidity of the atmosphere. This combination of ingredients makes the most terrific explosive propellent that is known in the world, as an agent of man.

Nitro-glycerine is perhaps a more powerful mixture; but it has not yet been brought under control.

Nearly every civilized nation manufactures its own gunpowder. In this country we have several large companies engaged in its manufacture, which at best is a very hazardous business. The powder made by our manufacturers, especially that made for sporting purposes, is generally of an excellent quality. I am unable to determine, either from my own experience or that of others, which American powder is the best.

Among the English manufacturers, Curtis & Hervey, J. Hall & Son, Pigou & Wilks, are celebrated. The principal American manufacturing companies are Hazard's, at Hazardville, Conn., the American Powder Co., the Oriental, Dupont's, and the Orange Powder Works.

I have used the Hazard powder because it suited me well; and having become acquainted with its force and quality, I have not felt any great desire to experiment with the powder made by other parties.

Some sportsmen are always on hand with a new article, praising its qualities and purity, and constantly comparing it with that made at other manufactories. I shall continue to use the Hazard till I am sure of finding a better powder.

Much is said about one powder being cleaner than another. Possibly there may be some difference in this respect, but hardly to that extent which many sportsmen imagine. All of the very best is dirty enough to satisfy the most slovenly person that ever pulled a trigger.

But persons unacquainted with the different qualities of powder should remember it is almost impossible, even for those who are engaged in its manufacture, to tell, simply by looking at it, whether a powder is high-priced or not. At least, I never have been able to find any one who could. Let it not be understood, however, that there is no difference in the quality and purity of gunpowder; for I know there is plenty of very inferior stuff made, fit only for blasting purposes, but sometimes purchased as cheap powder for sporting use. The purchaser who pays twenty-five or thirty cents per pound for an article must not expect the quality to be of the best. But, in comparing the best qualities made by established manufacturers who have a reputation to keep, I do not think there is such a marked difference as many suppose.

For all kinds of shooting I prefer the unglazed powder. I always fear that the glazed is more or less leaded, to give it its beautiful gloss; and I know that it does not explode so quickly as that which is not glazed. There may, however, be some advantage in glazing powder which is to be shipped to foreign ports, especially in a warm climate.

The sportsman should study to know the kind and quantity of powder to be used in his gun; remembering that large-grained powder has more killing force, is much cleaner than the fine-grained, does not strain the gun so much, and produces less recoil. In my opinion, almost any gun can be made to shoot fairly, if the powder is well adapted, in respect to quality and grain, to the length and weight of the barrel. And, other things being equal, in proportion as the sportsman makes this subject a careful study will he excel in his performance with his gun.

At short distances, there is perhaps little difference between the effect of the coarse and fine powder; but at long distances, as in duck-shooting, the fine powder has no show. For this reason I have always used much larger powder than most sportsmen.

There are but few methods of testing the quality of gunpowder. The old-fashioned way of rubbing it on your finger-nail, or between your fingers, to see if there is any gritty feeling, does very well as far as it goes; and almost all good powder will bear this test. I have frequently tested gunpowder by means of a spring, used by the manufacturers for determining its strength. But I think this affords no fair criterion to judge by, unless the size of the grain be also considered.

The process of making gunpowder is thus given by Greener: —

"The three ingredients, (charcoal, nitre, and sulphur,) after being carefully weighed in their due proportions, are sifted into a large trough and well mixed together by the hands.

"They are then conveyed to the powder-mill. This is a large circular trough, having a smooth iron bed, on which two mill-stones are secured to a horizontal axis, and revolve, traversing each other, and making nine or ten revolutions a minute.

"The powder is mixed with a small quantity of water, put on the bed of the mill, and then kept subject to the pressure of the stones; and if we calculate the weight of the two mill-stones at six tons, it follows that in four or five hours' incorporation on this bed, it subjects the ingredients to the action of full ten thousand tons. It is this long-continued grinding, compounding, and blending together of the mixture that alone renders it useful and good.

"After this intimate mixing, it is conveyed away in the shape of mill-cake, and firmly pressed between plates of copper, and the mass is more compressed and in thinner cakes.

"It is then broken into small pieces with wooden mallets, and taken to the corning-house, where it is granulated by putting it into sieves, the bottoms of which are made of bullock's hide, prepared like parchment, and perforated with holes about two tenths of an inch in diameter. From twenty to thirty of these sieves are secured to a large frame, moving on an *eccentric* axis, or crank, of six inches' throw; two pieces of *lignum vitæ*, six inches in diameter, and two inches or more in thickness, are placed on the broken press-cakes in each sieve. The machinery is then put in rapid motion; the balls of *lignum vitæ* pressing upon the powder, and striking against the sides of the sieve, force it through the apertures in grains of various sizes on to the floor, from whence it is removed and again sifted through finer sieves of wire, to separate the dust and classify the grain.

"The grains afterwards undergo a process of glazing by friction against each other, in barrels containing nearly two hundred pounds, making forty revolutions per minute, and lasting several hours, according to the fancy of the purchaser. This part of the business I entirely disagree with, as injurious to quick and certain ignition.

"It is finally dried by an artificial temperature of 140° Fahrenheit; which is suffered gradually to decline.

"The last process is sifting it clear of dust, and then packing it in canisters or otherwise."

Gunpowder should always be kept in a close tin box or canister, and in a dry place, as dampness injures it by partial decomposition, besides somewhat impairing its quickness of combustion. When it has been exposed to dampness in the flask, it will regain much of its quickness and strength if dried over a fire. Or perhaps a safer way, if convenient, is to put it on an earthen plate, and set it in the sunlight for a few hours. If dried by a fire, it is better to place the plate on some bricks on the back part of the stove or range, and lay on the plate a medium quantity of powder at a time. The bricks should be placed upon that part of the stove where there is a gradual heat. It then dries evenly and thoroughly.

Do not leave it to the kitchen girl's care, unless you want to incur the expense of purchasing a new stove, as well as more powder. It will take but a few minutes to dry it thoroughly. The powder-flasks or cans should also be emptied of all powder and dirt, and then held over the fire with their tops open to admit the heat, and give an escape for the damp air. After they are well dried, fill again with the powder, cork them tight and put them away in a dry, safe place. The next time you have occasion to use your double-barrel, you will find she speaks promptly, and with full force.

HOW GUN-BARRELS ARE MADE, &c.

SO few people understand how gun-barrels are made, and so important is it for every sportsman to know all the principal facts involved in the manufacture of a weapon with which he has so much to do, that I am induced to give an abridged statement of some of the general methods adopted in the manufacture of gun-barrels. I shall not go into a detailed history of the gun, but I wish to allude to its primitive condition and use, in order that the progress in its improvements may be noted.

The first gun that we know of was a very rude affair, — a sort of hand-gun, and was invented by a nobleman of Milan named Billus. It consisted simply of an iron tube attached to a stick, and was known as the "fire-lock." In the reign of Henry VI. of England, this weapon was improved by the addition of a priming-pan, which at that time was thought to be a great invention, as the priming powder had heretofore been held in a hollow made in the barrel or tube itself. These guns had no stocks, or what would answer to those of the gun of the present day. The tube was fastened to a straight stick, which was held in the hand. The crooked handle or stock was the next step in the way of improvement, — a device of the German or Italian manufacturers. In England the trigger in use on the crossbow suggested the application of a similar arrangement to the gun, and the weapons thus improved were called "matchlocks." Ignition was secured by moving a lighted match to the pan containing the priming powder. Subsequently the Dutch invented an apparatus for striking fire by the friction of a little wheel of steel against a piece of iron pyrites, causing a spark to ignite the powder. Both of these devices for discharging the gun were cumbersome, as well as fatal to any precision in the use of the weapon. The next improvement in order was the invention of the flint-lock, which was introduced in the time of Elizabeth. This invention made the gun a very serviceable weapon, and for a long period no important improvement was made in its construction. In 1807 Rev. Mr. Forsyth invented the percussion-lock, which, with various modifications and improvements, has come into general use.

The double-barrelled shot-gun, when first constructed, was made with the barrels placed one above the other. These were arranged so as to revolve, and present the percussion to the hammer of the lock. This arrangement, however, made the gun unwieldy, and the next step consisted in attaching a lock to each barrel. The placing of the barrels side by side, as at present, followed this arrangement; and I think we may consider that the end of improvements, so far as the position of the barrels is concerned, has been reached.

This matter of placing the barrels is a question that has received a great deal of attention from gun manufacturers, and the principles that underlie the present arrangement are worth noticing. Both barrels being subject to the same line of sight, it follows that, as they are placed horizontally, the bore of each barrel must incline inwards. The extent of this inclination is such that in guns of good quality the shot from both barrels, supposing both barrels to be discharged simultaneously, would cross each other at the distance of about forty yards. It will be observed in all guns that the thickness of the barrels is much greater at the breech than at the muzzle; and in order to conform the inclination of the bore to the line of sight, it becomes necessary to so adjust the breech ends of the barrels that the proper convergence of each charge shall be secured. This result is secured by reducing the thickness of the breech of each barrel at the point of contact. The extent of the reduction is about one half the thickness of the breech of each barrel, leaving between the two bores of the barrels, when placed side by side, the thickness of the breech of one barrel. On account of this reduction of the thickness of the barrels at the breech, it is undesirable, to say the least, to discharge the two barrels simultaneously. In any gun the recoil would be unpleasant, while in the cheaper class of weapons the great strain of the simultaneous explosion is likely to be greater than the barrels can stand.

The materials of which the higher qualities of gun-barrels are made are worth knowing; and as I cannot be expected to add anything of value on this subject to the published statements of Mr. William Greener, in his various treatises on the science of gunnery, I shall content myself with quoting freely from his work entitled "GUNNERY IN 1858," a work I would recommend to every sportsman.

MATERIALS FOR GUN-BARRELS.

Mr. Greener says, in speaking of the difficulties that surround the supply of the materials for gun-barrels in England:—

"The improvement in the manufacture of gun-barrels depends on the quality of the iron entirely; for it would be a useless waste of time to endeavor to make a good barrel of inferior metal. Science and experience have worked a wonderful change in the mixture of the superior qualities of iron: we have had announcements of silver-steel barrels at *ten guineas a pair* in the rough, of Brescian steel barrels, carbonized iron, and I know not how many more descriptions of compounds of metals, to form the best material for high-priced barrels. We have now metal which, in the rod, cannot be sold for less than one shilling and twopence per pound: the iron for a pair of barrels thus costing sixteen shillings and fourpence. This is good; nay, more than good,—'t is excellent. But there is a dark side of the picture, over which I would fain draw a veil: but I must not. Belgium, France, Holland, and Germany are improving, are marching onward, and we, alas! are standing still. Competition and cheapness combined are driving our gun trade into a labyrinth, out of which it will be long ere it finds the clew of exit. Our manufacture of inferior gunnery has certainly reached a depth of inferiority which never any other manufacture in the world reached, and I hope never will.

"During the existence of the slave-trade, many thousand guns 'per year were made of what is, by the trade, technically termed *park paling*, a material only fit for such purposes; and the cost of it was only *seven shillings and sixpence* each *spike;* but now we can furnish slave-traders with ship-loads, if they choose, at only *six shillings and sixpence* each, and it is still supposed that one of these *imitation* guns is the bloodmoney for a fellow-creature. It would be a just and equitable law, if our legislature would pass it, 'that every man should fire the guns he manufactures': nothing would more surely tend to improve the quality of guns of a low grade.

"A considerable increasing difficulty attends the obtaining of horse-nail studs from the continent. In various continental markets from whence we draw our supply, the skill and ability of the gun-barrel makers have increased; and the preference for superior firearms which is gaining ground with many continental sportsmen, has taught foreigners the value of their old horse-nails; and hence their increased scarcity. The inferior iron of which we make horse-nails prevents entirely the use of our own; consequently it requires no foresight to predict that our manufacturers will soon resolve themselves into two descriptions, — the very best and the very worst. The latter are already actively employed, and the others are advancing; as no doubt an increasing desire to obtain the most perfect gun pervades the thinking and affluent portion of the sporting world. . . . . .

"The iron ore of Great Britain is, beyond a doubt, inferior to that of many parts of the world; as all attempts to produce good steel from it have been attended ultimately with disappointment. Mr. Mushet, in his excellent work on iron says: 'The successful exertions of individuals have increased the manufacture of cast and malleable iron beyond all precedent in this country; nor have we been without some enlightened individuals, who have laudably endeavored to form a superior quality along with the extension of their manufactures. Success has so far crowned their praiseworthy exertions, aided by the operation of knowledge, in removing the prejudices of the artisan, that bar iron of our own manufacturing has been substituted, to a great extent, in place of that formerly used of the Swedish and Russian marks; but hitherto all attempts have failed to make bars of proper quality to form steel, in any degree comparable to that we daily manufacture in great quantities from foreign iron. . . . . .

"'The rapid progressive rise in value of this iron, for many years past, has already nearly doubled the price of steel to the workman, and given the trade in general a melancholy foretaste of the evils of dependence and *monopoly*.' So it is with the scrap, requisite to form good iron for gun-barrels."

COUNTERFEIT BARRELS.

"I have had several pairs of barrels sent from Berlin and Vienna, to be fitted up in the English style, with a certain knowledge that they were wanted for patterns; and in justice let it be said, the material and figure in the barrel were most beautiful: being a variety of Damascus, or fancy pattern in the metal, *superior* to anything seen of this country's manufacture. True, this is not an essential requisite, being more for appearance than utility; but the fact clearly shows the industry and will of the artisan. The iron, too, in clearness and density, we can scarcely surpass; therefore, if I regret that we are not advancing with our competitors, it proceeds from a clear conviction of the truth that we are slumbering upon our fancied superiority. A friend who had lately visited Liege, informed me that in one gun-maker's shop alone were employed fourteen of our best workmen; in fact he brought with him a gun which attests the great improvement the Belgians have made of late years. I have had possession of three guns, bearing on the lock and barrels, 'Joseph Manton, London'; 'Joseph Egg, London'; and 'John Manton & Son, London'; all of which were manufactured in Belgium; and so well is the imitation executed, that it would puzzle most amateurs to discover the fraud."

Laminated Steel.

"I make my own laminated steel: the difference in silver steel and common twist steel merely consists in the variety of tortuous twisting the former undergoes, while the latter is rolled out into rods of 6-16ths broad, with the fibres running perfectly longitudinal. The method of making or welding the pieces into a bloom is in the following way: Having collected a sufficiency of mild steel scraps, such as cuttings of saws, waste from steel-pen making, old coach springs, and the immense variety of pieces arising from the various manufactures of tools, they are cut into pieces of equal dimensions, polished in a revolving drum by their friction on each other, until quite bright, and then placed for fusion on the bed of an air furnace. The parts first fused are gathered on the end of a similarly fabricated rod, in a welding state, and these gather together, by their adhesion, the remainder as they become sufficiently heated, until the bloom is complete. The steel is then removed from the furnace, and undergoes the effect of a three-ton forge hammer and the tilt, until it forms a large square bar; it is then re-heated, and thence conveyed to the rolling mill, where eventually it is reduced to the size of rod required. I generally have the metal required cut into short pieces of six inches long. A certain number are bundled together and welded, and then drawn down again in the rolling mill. This can be repeated any number of times,—elongating the fibres and multiplying their number to an indefinite extent as may be required.

"The great advantage derived in this instance from air-furnace welding is a chemical one; for while the small pieces of steel are fusing on the bed of the air furnace, the oxygen is extracting the carbon, and leaves the resulting metal mild steel, or iron of the densest description; while the succeeding hammering and rolling and re-welding produce the mechanical arrangement of making the whole of an extremely fibrous description. The polishing secures a clean metal; indeed, so free from specks are the generality of barrels thus made, that it is scarcely possible to imagine clearer metal. When contrasted with the best of ordinary iron, by a powerful microscope, the closeness and density of grain are strongly apparent.

"To such an extent has this been carried, that I can produce specimens of a considerably increased specific gravity. The barrels made of this metal, in general, beat all tried against them; with this great advantage, that the finer the polish in the interior the better they shoot, and continue longer free from lead. The only difficulty is in the working; as the boring, filing, &c., are more difficult. Moreover, greater care is required to see that they are not annealed, when in the hands of the borer or filer; for in such case they would be considerably injured, though not to the same extent as barrels of a softer nature. I tested a great variety of bars by drawing them asunder longitudinally by the testing machine, and the average strength of a rod of 6-16ths broad by 5-16ths thick and 12 inches long, containing 1.40625 solid inches of iron, was equal to a tension of 11,200 lbs. This furnished a barrel having a thickness of metal in all parts of the arch equal, or 3·16ths of an inch thick, capable of bearing an internal pressure of 6,022 lbs. to the inch of the tube."

Barrel Figure.

"The generality of barrel makers spoil their metal by an attempt to obtain figure; for all extreme twistings in the rod depreciate the metal, by separating the fibres; to borrow a simile, they obtain only an overtwisted rope. This is not only disadvantageous, but useless; for the extreme density of the metal renders the figure difficult to be shown distinctly, as acid acts upon it but slightly, and never so well as on metal fabricated from two differently constructed carbonized materials.

"Many conjectures have been advanced, and an endless discussion created, to account for the watering or '*jowher*' in Oriental sword-blades, and genuine Damascus gun-barrels. Anything approaching the truth is seldom met with; though I think the explanation is very simple. It must be well known that there is an immense variety of different qualities in both iron and steel; no uniformity of quality is found in two productions out of a hundred. The very ore, the coal, the presence of oxygen, the excess of it, all vary the quality of the material. An excess of carbon is more detrimental than a scarcity; for where carbon has once been, it leaves an indelible mark, and though extracted to as great an extent as practicable, it leaves a residue that possesses an affinity to absorb carbon again equal to the original quantity: thus, steel once made will never, by any process yet known, be reconverted back to iron of the same nature it was originally. . . . .

"The original barrel-welders, the real Damascus iron-workers, were, like some of ours of the present day, not the most *conscientious* individuals, nor the most honorable. For, strange to say, — but it is not more strange than true, — on examination of most real Damascus barrels to be met with, we find the iron must have been so valuable as to induce the workmen *to plate* or *veneer* the superior mixture over a body of the commonest iron: all large barrels are thus made, rifles especially. I presume the moderns *borrowed* the invention; and it would be well if they made no more extensive use of it than on rifle barrels."

WIRE-TWIST AND DAMASCUS IRON.

"The modern method of making wire-twist and Damascus iron, being gradations from the same material, are here described under one head: —

"Alternate bars of iron and steel are placed on each other, in numbers of six each; they are then forged into one body or bar; after which, if for the making of wire-twist barrels, they are rolled down into rods of 3-8ths of an inch in breadth, varying in thickness according to the size of the barrel for which they are wanted: if for Damascus, invariably 3-8ths of an inch square. When about to be twisted into spirals for barrels, care must be taken that the edges of the steel and iron shall be outermost; so that when the barrel is finished and browned it shall have the appearance of being welded of pieces the size of wires, the whole length of the barrel. A portion of the rod, pickled in sulphuric acid, exhibits the following appearance, the bright parts being the steel, the other the iron.

When about to be converted into Damascus, the rod is heated the whole length, and the two square ends put into the heads (one of which is a fixture) of a kind of lathe, which is worked by a handle similar to a winch. It is then twisted like a rope (or, as Colonel Hawker says, wrung as wet clothes are) until it has from twelve to fourteen complete turns in the inch, when it presents this appearance.

By this severe twisting, the rod of six feet is shortened to three, doubled in thickness, and made perfectly round. Three of these rods are then placed together, with the inclinations of the twists running in opposite directions; they are then welded into one, and rolled down into a rod 11-16ths of an inch in breadth. Being pickled in acid, to eat away the iron, it exhibits the following appearance : —

This iron has long been held in great esteem. It looks pretty, but certainly does not possess either the strength or tenacity of wire-twist iron. It is well known that the strength of a rope may be destroyed by twisting it too much : so is it with this sort of iron. Iron is best when not twisted at all : I speak of the bar. It resembles wood, inasmuch as the strands or fibres run parallel, firmly adhere, and add strength to each other ; if you twist those fibres you tear them asunder, and they no longer support each other. So it is with iron.

"The objection made to the wire-twist is, that owing to the iron and steel being perfectly separate bodies running through the whole thickness of the barrel, there is a difficulty in welding them perfectly ; and of course there is danger of their breaking across, at any trifling imperfection or mis-weld. This objection is certainly well grounded, as many barrels break in the proving. I have seen a very strong barrel indeed broken across the knee without the slightest difficulty, while, to all appearance, it was perfectly sound. This is the reason why the manufacturers have ceased to make them, except for the American trade.

"It may be said that the fibres in the Damascus, after being torn asunder, are welded anew. True, but could you ever glue the fibres of a piece of wood (twisted in the same way) together again, to make them as strong as before? No, cut several pieces of wood across the grain and glue them together, you would not expect them, though equal in substance with a piece in which the grains run lengthwise, to be of equal strength. In short, I hold a Damascus barrel to be little superior to a common barrel, in which the fibres run parallel to the bore.

"All the varieties of figured barrels are but modifications of Damascus. The most endless variety possible may be attained; a figure with the carbonized material, showing only the ends or edges of the various laminæ, or portions of the face of that laminæ, may with equal facility be obtained, if the patience of the artist be in proportion. It would be a never-ending task, a subject for many volumes, to endeavor to describe a tithe of the varieties that might be, and have been made.

"The Belgians are very expert at this sort of ornamental work. The very minute Damascus figure they frequently produce is admirable, if beauty alone were the advantage sought in a gun-barrel. They use thirty-two alternate bars of steel and iron, and roll them into a sheet of 3-16ths thick, and then slit them by a machine into square rods; these are twisted in the way just described, but to such an extreme as to resemble the threads of a very fine screw: six of them are welded into one, instead of three as with us. The figure is so extremely fine as to appear not to be larger than the finest needle. I have seen barrels made in Liege, superior in minute figure to any real Damascus barrel, or sword either. Our workmen here say the steel is better; which I am inclined to think is true: it is a branch of the gun manufacture they have long excelled in. The very best 'Damascene' workers are to be found at La Chafontaine, a few miles from Liege, where they dwell in as beautiful a dell as fancy could wish, with a powerful hill-stream working their boring and grinding mills, thus enabling them to send their barrels into Liege, ready for the filer. I have spent considerable time, and taken great trouble, to produce in Birmingham iron equally good; and I have succeeded; but, unfortunately, Englishmen are so extravagant in their ideas of value, as to render the constant manufacture of this iron here a losing speculation. It can, however, be obtained from Belgium now, under the amended tariff, at ten per cent on the value. It can be purchased there, ready for barrel-making, at a franc per pound; and cheap it is at that price: two and a half francs would not purchase it here.

"That Damascus iron is incompatible with goodness, I can and shall clearly prove. Experiment with the testing machine shows a rod of wire-twist 3-8ths square, containing 1.6875 solid inches, as equal to a tension of 11,200 lbs.; whereas a rod, when converted into Damascus of 11-16ths of an inch in breadth, by 4-16ths in thickness, containing 2.625 solid inches, was only equal to 8,960 lbs.; thus showing a clear loss of full thirty-five per cent. And when welded into barrels of the dimensions described, the relative internal strength of each is 5,019½ lbs., and 3,292 lbs. *to the inch of tube.* This constitutes a great difference. But unfortunately that is not all.

"In the preceding chapter I noted the fact that all sorts of iron lose a portion of their strength by being heated or softened; but I found that Damascus suffered more than any other sort of iron, excepting the common kinds. For instance, the bar of wire-twist would, in the state it came from the rolling-mill, bear 11,200 lbs., but, after softening, it would only bear 10,180 lbs., being a diminution of 10 per cent. A bar of Damascus suspending a weight of 8,940 lbs., the measure of its strength when annealed, was 7,840 lbs., being a falling off of 12½ per cent. Thus, I trust I have clearly shown, that whatever other quality Damascus possesses, strength is not one of its properties. It must not, however, be supposed that the above weight indicates its greatest strength; on the contrary, its strength can be increased full 22½ per cent by cold hammering. Still, however, it will only hold its relative position to other kinds of iron with respect to strength, since they are all capable of having their strength increased by the same process.

"Damascus barrels have fallen much into disuse, being rarely seen except as pistol barrels, which, together with a great quantity of *counterfeits*, are made for the South and North American trades, in the shape of double and single guns of a flashy appearance, —

HOW GUN-BARRELS ARE MADE. 221

all invariably *veneered* or *plated* with ribbons of this ornamental iron. I shall now dismiss this subject; after remarking, that certainly a very handsome barrel may be made after this principle, if too much twisting be avoided. It has been seen that the rods are twisted until there are fourteen turns in the inch of length: an excess productive of the detrimental effect mentioned; while, had there been but two turns, a large proportion of strength, if not all, would have been retained. One turn only, under the same circumstances, would very likely be highly beneficial; indeed I have found it to be so: one twist binds the interior strands, as the outer does the interior in a rope, and thus adds strength. This shows that there is a medium in all things."

Horse-Shoe Nails.

" The use of old horse-shoe nails is of a date nearly coeval with the use of small fire-arms. These nails are made from rod iron of the best description; and the hammering cold, or tempering the nail, so benefits and condenses the iron as to improve it greatly. The method in use until a late period was to fill and force into an iron hoop, of six or seven inches diameter, as many stubs as it would contain, to weld the whole, and draw them down to a bar of such dimensions as might be required. Modern improvement, however, has shown the advantage of cleansing the stubs perfectly by a revolving drum, and then fusing and gathering them into a *bloom* on the bed of an air furnace. Thus a body of from 40 to 50 lbs. of melting iron can be obtained at one heat; a matter of economy and necessity, where large quantities are required, besides possessing the superior advantage of having the whole mass equally heated : this cannot be done by the old hoop method, as the surface must be frequently burnt before the interior is at all in a welding state."

Stub Iron and Steel.

"Experience taught the late Mr. Adams and his brother George — who still manufacture some of the best gun iron in the world — that the stub iron alone was insufficient; for even then (forty years ago) the absurdity of imagining that no barrels were or could be good without being soft, was understood and acted upon by them. They introduced at first one fourth of steel to three of stubs; this having been found highly advantageous, the prejudices of the gun-makers were gradually overcome, or left in abeyance from ignorance of the introduction. It is a fact that as late as 1842, when I issued my former work, men who had been all their lives *gun-makers* (by courtesy) actually refused to believe that any steel at all entered into the composition of the best barrels; and several whom I know perfectly well ordered the factors with whom they dealt 'to be sure to send them no barrels with steel in, as they did not wish their customers' hands to be blown off.'

Charcoal iron has, up to this day, been the only

stub twist barrels they (and we believe two thirds of the provincial makers also) have ever been served with. Reason with these men, and they will snappishly tell you, 'We pay the best price, and we ought to have the best; we don't see that our neighbors have any better.' On one occasion of my calling upon one of the first provincial gun-makers in the kingdom, the subject of barrels was adverted to : 'An excellent work that of yours, I dare say; but, sir, you have done a deal of harm : it is wrong to let gentlemen know too much ; they give you far too much trouble ; they get too knowing.' These, and such like observations, are the only thanks I ever received from the generality of the gun trade. There are, however, some enlightened men who, understanding the subject, have appreciated my motives ; but by far the greater proportion have done the reverse, asserting 'that I had told them nothing but what they knew before.'

"The mixture of a portion of steel with the stubs having clearly shown an improvement, an increased proportion has been adopted by various makers ; we have had as high as three fourths of steel to one of iron. Where proper attention is paid to the clipping of the steel to pieces, corresponding with the stubs, and properly mixing the whole, welding and forging by the heavy hammer, reducing by a tilt and rolling down to the smallest description of rod, a most excellent, tenacious, and dense body of iron is thus obtained ; while, by cutting into lengths of six inches, bundling a number together, and re-welding them into a bar, an increased density and tenacity is gained, by an increase in quantity, and an elongation of the fibrous system. Any description of barrel, of this iron, if made with a moderate degree of care and attention, is considerably stronger than any explosive fluid ever yet compounded could burst, under any circumstances bordering on *fair experiment.*

" The great advantage derived from welding on the bed of an air furnace, arises from an absence of the minute portions of charcoal, of either wood or coal, as the case may be. Millions of these very minute portions are imbedded in the midst of the metal in every part. They are enclosed in cells originally of their own dimensions, but are drawn out with the fibres to an indefinite extent, forming a system of tubes that may be compared to the capillary system in trees, and making the iron of a spongy, compressible nature. It is the absence of these particles of charcoal that gives part of the superiority to steel as now made for gun-barrels; and the existence of a portion of them causes the inferiority of all other kinds of iron. In a chemical analysis of iron, a large portion of crude coal-charcoal or wood-charcoal is found, according as either has been used during the manufacture. This is not of course given as so much carbon in the result, though the injury is equally detrimental as an excess of carbon is to the goodness of the metal; for it renders the whole porous, and liable to attract moisture and induce oxidation. It must be kept prominently in view, and clearly comprehended that the denser the body of metal, the less the liability to oxidize, or in other words *rust;* and here is the one great preservative principle in good iron: 'it is the fibre of dense cocoa-wood, compared with that of willow or saugh.' In all situations and for all purposes, where iron is liable to sudden changes of either heat or cold, wet or dry, the very best of iron should be obtained; as it will be less affected by the changes of temperature, and amply repay by its durability the extra cost in the first instance. . . . .

" The frequent welding and re-rolling of iron is of the most beneficial tendency, the elongation of the fibres being highly advantageous; for a fibrous piece of iron may be compared to a wire rope, the more strands the greater tenacity; and the smaller the strands, even up to a proximity of fineness to the human hair, the greater the weight they will bear in tension. One large wire which, when single, will suspend 500 lbs., will, when drawn down to six small ones, suspend 600 lbs.; and so on to the greatest extreme. Another great advantage received by the repeated reworking of iron is obtaining an increased density; for when this is secured to a certain extent, you have closed in proportion the pores of the metal; and in this state it is not liable to that degree of expansion or contraction, or that fluctuation in strength, which arises from softening the iron. Nor can you gain, save to a limited extent, any improvement by hammering,— hammer-hardening, for instance, — simply because it is already improved to the utmost extent we are at present acquainted with."

Mr. Greener explains quite fully how the various

kinds of cheap barrel iron are made, such as "charcoal iron," "three-penny skelp iron," "sham damn skelp," &c.; but as I assume that none of my readers care to own a weapon made of such materials, I will not quote the particulars of their manufacture, but pass to his remarks on barrel-making.

Welding.

The welding of the rods of barrel iron into barrels, is described by Mr. Greener thus:—

"The metal rods are twisted by means of two iron bars, the one fixed, the other loose. In the latter there is a prong or notch to receive one end; and when inserted, the bar is turned by a handle. The fixed bar preventing the rod from going round, it is bent and twisted over the movable rod like the pieces of leather round the handle of a whip. The loose bar is unshipped, the spiral knocked off, and the same process recommenced with another rod. The length of all the spirals depends on the breadth of the rod: for instance, the stub-twist has sixteen circles in six inches long; a rod of five feet will make a spiral of only seven inches; while iron, of an inch in breadth, will make a spiral of as many inches long as there are twists: hence the reason why best barrels have more joinings than common ones of equal length.

"The Damascus, being rolled into rods of 11-16ths broad, forms a spiral with the appearance shown in the accompanying woodcut.

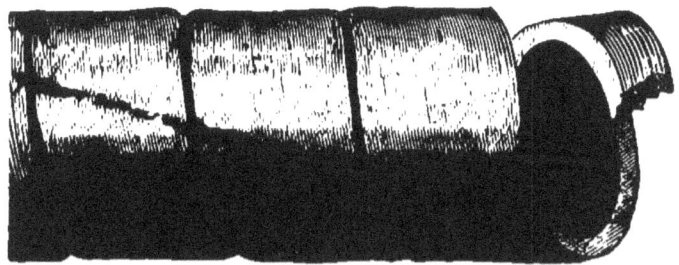

"The fancy steel barrels and others, where the rod is formed of more than one piece, such as the stub Damascus, &c., is of rather greater breadth, like the representation below.

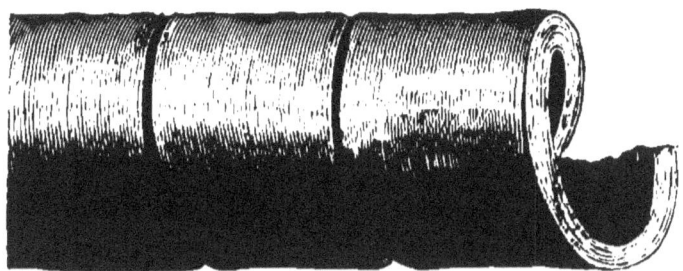

"The iron made from stubs and steel, and plain fibrous steel, is invariably rolled down into rods of 6-16ths broad, forming a spiral, as below.

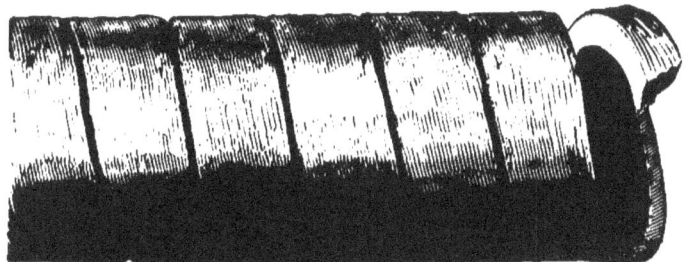

"A proper attention to the fineness of the spiral will always enable an amateur to detect any attempt at imposition. . . . .

"The spirals being formed, the welders commence their day's work. The batch consists of a foreman, one on whose skill all depends, and two subordinates, whose duty it is to blow the bellows, strike, &c.

"They proceed in the first place to weld probably a dozen long common barrels for the American trade; which are generally composed of the inferior iron mentioned before, rolled into two lengths of different thicknesses. These skelps are heated, and beaten on a groove until they form a tube half closed. They are then heated again, and closed with one edge overlapping the other; as a brazier would overlap the edge of a tin pipe for boys to blow peas with.

"They then commence the welding of twist barrels. Spirals that are intended for the breech end are heated to a welding heat for about three inches, removed from the fire, and jumped close by striking the end against the anvil. Again they are heated, and again jumped, to insure the perfect welding. They are then beaten lightly in a groove, to make them round. The neatest part of the process consists in the joining of the points of the two rods, so as to make the barrel appear as if it had been twisted out of one rod. The ends of the two rods are a little detached, brought from the fire, and applied to each other; a gentle tap is then given, and the union is perfect in an instant. The rapidity and dexterity with which this is accomplished, ought to be seen to be duly appreciated. This trouble is only taken with the best barrels. In the manufacture of barrels of an inferior description, the ends of the rods are cut in a sloping direction, and, when welded together, become quite square at the part where the pieces are joined. In a finished barrel the points of junction are easily recognized. By tracing the twist, a confusion will be found to exist for about an eighth of an inch, every six or seven inches; and from this appearance you may conclude that, for a barrel so joined, the welder had not the best price. Having joined the whole of the spirals, three inches are again heated to a welding heat, the mandril is introduced, and the tube hammered, in a groove, to the size required. This operation is repeated until the whole length is finished.

Then follows hammer-hardening: that is, beating the barrel, in a comparatively cold state, in a groove, with light hammers, for the space of half an hour. This is a most important part of the process. It closes the pores, condenses the texture of the metal, compresses a greater substance into less bounds, increases greatly the strength of the barrel, and renders it more elastic. Yet this is seldom done, unless specially requested; and then a gratuity is, of course, expected either in money or beer. A few pots of the juice of Sir John Barleycorn will infuse more strength into your barrels than you could purchase for ten times the amount in money; as they have the effect of making the hammers descend with increased velocity."

Boring and Grinding Gun-barrels.

The boring and grinding of the barrels is the process next in order, which Mr. Greener describes as follows:—

"Boring and grinding gun-barrels generally take place under the same roof; the borer occupying a very small shop, the grinder a large one. Two men and two boys are generally found in a shop. There are four benches, to each a spindle, in which there is an oblong hole to receive the end of the boring bit. The barrel is secured on a sort of carriage, which is at liberty to traverse the whole length of the bench. A boring bit is then selected of suitable size; it is put into the spindle, and the point introduced into the end of the barrel. A sort of lever is then taken and hooked on to a kind of staple, or a piece of hooked iron (a number of which are fixed in one side of the bench the whole length), and passed behind the carriage to force it up to the bit; this is removed and fixed again, until, by forcing up the carriage, the boring bit has passed through the whole of the barrel. During this operation a stream of water is kept playing on the barrel to keep it cool. A bit, of larger dimensions, is next introduced and passed through; then others of still larger dimensions, until the whole of the scales or blacks are entirely bored out; or until the barrel has become so large in the bore, as to preclude any further boring with safety. If the scales are of great extent, the fault is the forger's, and the loss will consequently be his. If the barrels be found perfect, they are sent back to the filer, or he comes to inspect them, in order to ascertain whether they be perfectly straight in the inside; if not, to make them so.

"The necessity of great care and attention to this point must be very obvious; for, if not perfectly correct at this stage, it will require more skill and time to get it correct afterwards than the generality of barrel-makers are inclined to bestow.

"When the inside has been found to be all right, the barrel is ready for grinding. Many barrel-makers turn their barrels entirely by self-acting lathes, and thus obtain a correct taper from breech end to muzzle. Experience has clearly convinced us that this is not the best shape, but slightly hollow towards the muzzle is preferable, as additional weight there is decidedly injurious, and the shooting of barrels of lighter construction is decidedly better.

"The generality of Birmingham barrels are ground to the size required on large stones, which revolve at a terrific rate. The skill acquired by many of the workmen is astonishing. Over and over again have we seen barrels coming from the mill put into the lathe, and found almost as true as if they had been turned. They have a method of allowing the barrel to revolve in their hands at half the rate of the stone, and by this means they grind them so fine that many would be puzzled to determine whether they had been turned or ground, were the barrel smoothed lengthways merely to take out the marks of the stone. We have seen the squares of a rifle barrel ground to as perfect an octagon as the eye could assist in forming. Best barrels are generally turned after they are ground. Inferior barrels are struck up with a large rubber, or smooth, by boys; in some instances by women."

The Patent Breech.

"The invention of the patent breech," says Mr. Greener, "was the emanation of a scientific mind; for it has been productive of more real benefit to the progress of gunnery than any other improvement of the last two centuries. Experience and study in the theory of guns and gunpowder give the mind a much more enlarged view of the subject, if regulated by the established laws of true and sound principles: a want of thorough knowledge induces the individual to draw conclusions prematurely, and thus he is apt to fall, and to lead others, into error. I confess, that, together with many hundreds more, I once concluded that the great advantage of the patent breech arose entirely from the loose state in which the powder was preserved while in the breech, and its thus being more instantaneously ignited. But I have already shown that the quickness of powder is, in a great measure, the greatest drawback to its efficacy, and I am clearly convinced that compression, in most instances, is beneficial, by retarding the ignition to a certain extent. Here, then, is proof positive, that we have been on the wrong scent, and running after a 'Will o' the Wisp.'

"There is the clearest evidence that the only advantage to be derived from any conical form of breech does not arise from any peculiarity attached to the ignition of the gunpowder, but solely from the effect of the angular shape; conical form being best suited, or presenting the least direct surface, to the action of the exploded fluid: the angles receive the blow and throw it off at the same opposite angle, and so on, without receiving any amount of force from the element striking it, and thus the elastic fluid is enabled to be resisted efficaciously. The cone becomes and

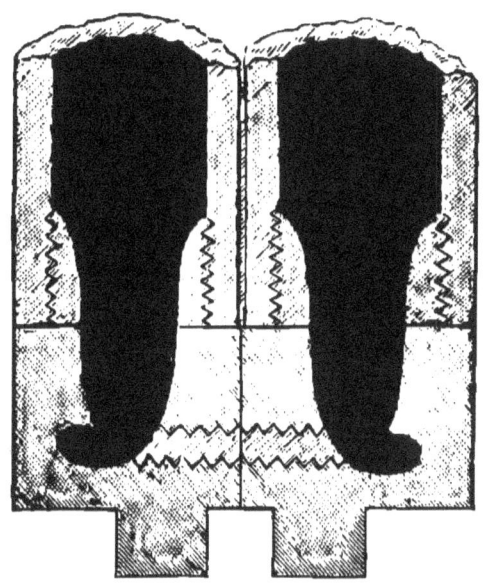

forms an artificial solid base, to a certain extent; and as such, it is much more beneficial than the same quantity of powder ignited on a flat surface, — as a common plug breech, for instance; for here the direct quantity of space on the face of the breech receives the same impulse as the ball projected, and is acted upon in precisely the same ratio in proportion to their different weights. In a musket of 11 lbs., the comparative weight of gun and ball is as 1 to 176; and exactly in that proportion will be the distribution of impulse from the expellent fluid. It thus becomes a plain question between the patent breech and the flat surface of the plug. The two halves of a parabola inverted, or the shape of a parabolic spindle, will be the best shape, according to the laws of science. The representation given on page 234 is as near as I can get the engraver to represent my views of the best shape of breech."

Laminated Steel Barrels.

With reference to laminated steel barrels, Mr. Greener says:—

"There are six qualities or varieties of mixtures of iron for barrels of best quality. The plate-facing contains two kinds finished, composed of steel entirely, but of different degrees of carbonization: one is composed entirely of a laminated series containing many scores of distinct laminæ in the thickness of the sides of the barrels, twisted and beat into tortuous shapes; the other, of larger laminæ, but showing the edges of the laminæ at an angle with the length, and thus appearing larger than if presenting the side or end of the plates.

"Care must be taken that the great proportion of the

fibres shall always run round the tube, so that the greatest portion of strength may be obtained, together with a beautiful figure. The cost of this arrangement is considerable, as it involves a great waste of metal, and occupies a considerable time to work and re-work, — twisting, fagoting with the bars placed in various forms, at acute angles to each other, at right angles plaiting three or four rods together, as a lady does her hair, cutting these into pieces, fagoting and welding them into one, and, in short, undergoing an endless routine of manipulations, which it would be strictly unprofitable to detail, but are all productive of cost. An ingenious man may work and improve metal of this nature until its cost equals the price of silver; and, if judiciously done, improving it still, even until he has wasted 90 per cent of the original material.

"The ultimate characteristics and properties of iron have, as yet, never been ascertained: it is capable of being condensed until it becomes nearly, if not quite, equal to the specific gravity of silver or lead. No pursuit, mechanical or philosophical, presents so great and so beneficial a research, to the whole civilized and scientific world, as iron. I could twist and retwist iron, until, from the beautiful and interesting results, it would become with me a sort of monomania. I wonder not at the variety of patterns in a Damascus sword-blade: the mind conveys me to the scene, and a regret arises that I did not live in those times; yet still it is but a mechanical arrangement, directed by an ingenious mind, and the ultimate benefit, apart from the beauty, is no more than imaginary. However, it proves that the Orientals were artists, and that they were appreciated: were this the case now with us, we could do all they ever did, and more.

"Laminated steel is now a great fact. It is a name stereotyped in Belgium, Germany, France, and America, as well as in the place of its birth, — England; and orders come from all parts of the globe for the celebrated laminated steel. Every writer of eminence is loud in its praise, and justly so too; for about its merits there is no mistake. No combination of metals ever yet before tried since the birth of gunnery can equal it, either in density, ductility, or tenacity. A laminated steel barrel has never been known to burst. 'Reputed' laminated steel barrels have been burst, but no real one ever. Nor is it probable, save from malconstruction. Through inattention in the welding the best of metal may be burnt; but the better the iron, the greater the difficulty. Steel is more liable to melt than burn; so that, with care and skill on the part of the workman, it will very seldom indeed occur. But that chance is provided for, as far as human judgment can do, in intrusting such barrels only to first-rate and steady workmen. Such men are no doubt, to a certain extent, scarce; but they may yet be found; the Birmingham welder of proved skill and ability is inferior to none in the world. Laminated steel barrels are more scarce than welders.

"Although the various manufacturers of Europe have complimented me by adopting the name of my invention, yet I am sorry to add it is but in name;

there are very few even tolerable imitations of them. The cost is the 'bugbear'; the name costs nothing, and can easily be assumed; but to make laminated steel barrels is quite another matter: it touches the pocket, and interferes with the profit; and it is only in very rare cases indeed — although the order may be as explicit as words can make it — that the real article is supplied. There are very few makers in Birmingham who in reality make 'laminated steel.' Steel barrels are more plentiful: they care not so much for the price of the metal; it is the after repeated manipulations that are evaded: the labor and loss of material is too much, and is necessarily 'shirked,' and argument is always met with the answer, 'We see nothing in it.' Yet the words 'laminated steel' are to be found engraved upon barrels of the lowest quality of iron of which double barrels are made. Iron twist is subjected to a similar process to that already described as employed in producing Damascus iron, and which may be termed common iron Damascus. Thousands of guns are made from this kind of metal, and yearly sent to the United States of America; yet all are unblushingly represented as 'laminated steel barrels.' The actual price charged for these sort of guns in the United States I know not, but have no doubt for the whole gun it is about equal to what would be the prime cost of a pair of real laminated steel barrels alone.

"Purchasers should be fully acquainted with the fact that it is impossible to produce laminated steel barrels at a low figure: labor, high-priced, skilled labor, is always costly; and talent must be paid for in all parts of the world. The attainment of high class barrels at a low figure, as a rule, is an impossibility; and the maker who would pretend, promise, or undertake to make a laminated steel barrelled gun under £15 to £20 is an arrant deceiver: he could never profitably carry out such an intention, even if he possessed the ability to produce the article. For judgment, skill, and ability, as well as labor, are required to produce laminated steel barrels. Steel alone is not laminated; and that is another difficulty: fortunately there are not many persons capable of effecting it. My method of laminating steel is kept as much out of sight as possible, as a means of self-protection."

On the subjects of gun-locks and the percussioning of a gun, I do not deem it necessary to speak particularly. Good barrels are usually not at fault in these particulars; and if the remarks I have so liberally quoted from Mr. Greener, with reference to the composition and manufacture of gun-barrels, shall be the means of warning any of my readers against many of the cheap and unsafe guns that are only too plentiful in our market, I shall feel that I have surrendered my pages to good purpose.

Steel Barrels for Shot Guns.

I have recently heard of a new process for making gun-barrels, which, if successful in producing barrels satisfactory in every respect, is certainly an improvement upon the present established process of manufacturing them.

The process to which I refer consists in taking, in the first place, a piece of decarbonized steel, of very fine quality, and large enough to make a barrel of the required length, and puncturing a hole through it. A mandril or piston, of the size of the bore required, is then placed in the hole, when the steel, by some powerful means, is drawn over or around it. I am not acquainted with all the particulars of this new process, and can therefore give only the general principles involved. I will add that I think the process a practicable one. I know that barrels have been made in the way described, and I see no reason why the process should not be successful. Certain it is that decarbonized steel can be easily manipulated, and the working of it over a mandril or piston would seem likely to insure a bore of greater uniformity than the old process. Then, too, the material of the barrels is superior to that now used even in the best guns. It is much stronger than iron, and barrels made of it are therefore better adapted to stand the strain put upon all guns when discharged.

PIGEON-SHOOTING.

THE shooting of wild and domestic pigeons is a practice well calculated to increase the sportsman's skill in shooting on the wing, and especially in making snap-shots.

This kind of sport is conducted by clubs and associations, for the purpose of giving members opportunities to shoot at flying birds, and it is practised more in the Western and Middle than in the Eastern States. Owing to the want of efficient game-laws, or the laxity with which those already existing in some of the States are enforced, game is constantly becoming scarce throughout the country; and, in my opinion, the art of shooting on the wing must be entirely given up in some sections, unless the game laws be made more effective. Should the former result occur, pigeon-shooting will be the only kind of sport left for those who love to pull the trigger. Even now, in some large cities and towns of the Eastern States, the expert who wishes to try his new gun, or the novice desirous of testing his progress in the art, must go to the shooting-club, if he would be sure of finding game.

Seldom will the sportsman have a more trying occasion for his nerves, seldom will he have greater need of all his coolness and quickness combined, than when at the stand in his first pigeon-shoot. Many an excellent shot, on his first appearance at one of these shoots, and walking up to his position before the trap, surrounded by a crowd of spectators, will find himself unable wholly to conceal a slight tremulous feeling. Many a hunter, who in the field is as firm as a rock, will, under these circumstances, knowing that his standing will be affected by the result of his shot, show the white feather somewhat, until by practice he has learned to overcome his nervous excitement. And it is often noticed that many who in the brush can knock over their game-birds, one with each barrel, in handsome style, make but a poor tally on coming to the pigeon-shoot.

One of the greatest mistakes made by sportsmen in their first attempts at pigeon-shooting is *holding on to the bird too long*, thus letting him get out of killing range. This is especially apt to be the case while the bird is flying from the shooter. The mark then is not only a small one to hit, but the vulnerable part of the bird is not presented to the marksman. The shooter may, and generally will, *hit* his pigeon, but often, in such cases, it will get over the boundary line. The great secret in killing pigeons from a ground-trap is to shoot them the instant they rise, and before they have got under full headway. If they are coming toward you on a quarter shot, either to the left or right, there is no need of haste. But otherwise, the sooner the bird is well covered by the gun, the more likely will you be to hear the referee call out, "Dead bird."

The arrangements for a pigeon-shoot are usually

made in a large open field, if possible without trees or buildings within its enclosure. Near the centre is placed the trap or traps, and around this centre is made a circle one hundred and sixty yards in diameter.

The circle is marked by stakes bearing a white or red flag. Numbers, from one to the number of those who intend to shoot, are written upon pieces of paper, or, more usually, upon a cut wad, and put into a hat. "Before taken," it is "well shaken," — each person drawing his number, and taking his position accordingly. No. 1 takes his stand at the trap, and will shoot first, No. 2 coming next. As soon as No. 1 has made his shot, he falls into the circle in his order, at the rear of the highest number. In this manner they "swing round the circle," taking their turns at the trap in rotation.

When two traps are used, they are marked H. and T., meaning *Head* and *Tail*, and a piece of coin is turned, to decide from which trap the bird shall fly and be shot at. By this simple regulation sportsmen will be likely to have fair play, and at the same time not be likely to have their pigeons "doctored," by the tail and wing feathers being pulled out, as is sometimes done by the initiated.

When all is ready, No. 1, whose stand is at the trap, gives the word *pull*, and the trap is sprung by a man whose business is to "tend the trap," and the bird is let out. The shooter must keep the breech of his gun below the right elbow, until the bird rises. Often the pigeon will trouble the sportsman, by standing upon the ground for some moments before taking wing.

Should the bird be missed by the sportsman at the trap, and pass' the boundary line, he is stopped, if possible, by the nearest gun, as he passes over the circle of shooters. If the members of the club are all good shots, but few birds will escape.

The shooting-clubs of New England have, I believe, generally adopted the New York rules and regulations. I give in the Appendix their by-laws, and a form of constitution framed by a Boston club, to illustrate the plan in full.

CLOSING REMARKS.

IT is my desire that American sportsmen should take a high position in the science and art of shooting, a position becoming educated gentlemen; and that the imputations often cast upon sportsmanship, such as its being necessarily connected with bad habits and associations, be shown to be entirely unwarranted.

There is in this country a strong prejudice against the sporting fraternity; and this feeling has been carried so far that even to be seen with a gun is sometimes considered beneath the dignity of a gentleman. But, as before stated, very different ideas are entertained on the other side of the Atlantic. No English gentleman considers himself fully educated unless he possesses a knowledge of the manly art of shooting on the wing; and to be a crack shot is, with an Englishman, an honor not to be despised.

It is true we are in some respects differently situated from the English. We have not a nobility able to indulge in sporting and give character to it by social and legal prescription. But we have, nevertheless, among our better classes, sufficient taste and discretion, as well as sufficient leisure, to make hunting a pleasant and honorable recreation.

What is essential, in order to bring about this

CLOSING REMARKS. 245

desirable result, is the better education of our sportsmen in all matters connected with sporting, including the manufacture of the gun, the proper loading and handling and carrying of it. We must do away with the ignorance and awkwardness sure to be exhibited when these subjects are not studied in detail.

Every sportsman knows something about a gun; but if he has studied it no further than to know how to load it with certain charges, and then shoot with it, however well, he has but little knowledge of the scientific operations connected with the weapon itself.

The gun is an engine of greater variety and more exquisite mechanism than any other of its size. And to be able to use this engine well, one must know all its parts, and the devices for improving its working.

The study of the proportionate quantity of powder and shot best suited to the character of a gun, is of prime importance to the sportsman; and, although we seldom hear the subject discussed, yet out of a dozen fair shooters there will hardly be found two who load their guns exactly alike. Of course *all* cannot be correct in the proportions of powder and shot in their charges. Some sportsmen may say it is ridiculous to be so "fussy" about the loading of a gun. And yet these very persons will doubtless close up an argument on this subject with their "rules," thereby making a virtual acknowledgment of the necessity of a general rule. In previous pages I have given what I believe to be the standard rules for loading; and if $2\frac{3}{4}$ drachms of powder and $1\frac{1}{4}$ ounces of shot are the standard medium charge for any gun which weighs from 6½ to 7½ lbs., what shall be said of those who constantly shoot but 1½ drachms of powder with the same quantity of shot, or 1½ ounces of shot and 2 drachms of powder, or 3 drachms of powder with 1 ounce of shot? I know of sportsmen with whom each of these charges is a standard rule. They shoot indeed fairly with them; but in my opinion their guns if properly loaded would do much better.

Much remains to be learned before our knowledge of breech and muzzle loading shot guns can be considered complete. Attention is now strongly directed to this subject, and improvements in these weapons may reasonably be anticipated. Generally speaking, those in this country who have hitherto used the gun most have not been men of mechanical aptitude or of scientific acquirements. It therefore becomes those who love and understand the weapon best to be the pioneers in adopting or encouraging whatever improvements may be made in it. Let every one remember, too, that many of the greatest improvements in machinery have been suggested or devised by persons not directly engaged in the business for which the improvement was made.

Another point for the consideration of sportsmen, old or young, is the manner of carrying the gun. This is a point of no little consequence. The rules for carrying in the field have been laid down in the chapter "How to carry"; but I would here remark more particularly upon the manner of carrying in the

CLOSING REMARKS. 247

street, in the cars, or at a gathering for any kind of shooting.

A sportsman can tell at a glance, by noticing how a person handles and carries his gun, whether he is well up to his work in shooting. The poor shooter will usually be recognized, when walking, by his carrying his gun horizontally, at some distance from his body, and generally with half a yard or so of the meanest kind of a cloth gun-case hanging down from the muzzle; when at a shooting-gathering, by his carrying it on his shoulder, with the muzzle poking far out behind, so that every time he turns suddenly in the crowd, some one gets an ugly rap. At other times he appears with his gun heavily loaded, caps on and hammers down, — especially if he be a countryman, — ready to shoot at the trap or target, or perhaps at some companion if the gun should accidentally go off. Again he will be seen with the muzzles of his loaded gun resting on the ground, and his body leaning against the breech, or resting his arms or body on the muzzles of his loaded barrels in various careless ways. All these slovenly ways of carrying and handling guns may frequently be seen in any large collection of sportsmen, and being proofs of great ignorance or carelessness, they serve to indicate to the looker-on *who the poor shots are;* for no one can be an expert, excelling in any kind of artistic or mechanical employment, without showing a fitting elegance and ease of movement when about his business.

The attention of sportsmen should be especially directed to the needed improvements in cartridges for shot, applicable to both muzzle and breech loaders. I have already alluded to this subject in the chapter "About Shot"; and I hope that an improvement in this respect, so needful to increase the power and closeness of shooting, will be brought about, in a way that shall not only bring honor to the inventor, but compensate him with a remunerative patent.

Finally, I would urge upon my brother Nimrods the prime importance of keeping their guns clean and free from rust. The more I think of this subject, the more firmly I am convinced that, generally speaking, *guns do not wear out, but rust out.*

It is not necessary to weary the reader with a dissertation upon the importance of keeping the gun clean. Certainly, if a gun is worth having, it is worth keeping in good order. We want no further evidence that a person is a poor hunter, than the knowledge that he lets *rust run riot* in the fowling-piece, which he should carefully guard against all foulness. If it is a choice and expensive gun, so much the greater is the offence. A good gun has cost too much labor and too much money to be destroyed with rust. Even when using breech-loaders, much care is required to keep them clean, although cleansing may be done far more easily than in the muzzle-gun, because there is an opportunity of examining the entire length of the barrel inside, and of detecting the first symptoms of foulness or rust.

In conclusion, let the name of the American sportsman become honorably known throughout the world; and let us develop a taste for the various kinds of hunting in the field, such as becomes a great and intelligent people. Let us be as famous in the science and art of using the *shot-gun* "*on the wing*," as we have been the world over for our use of the Kentucky rifle.

11*

APPENDIX.

TECHNICAL NAMES USED BY GUN-MAKERS, THAT APPLY TO THE DIFFERENT PARTS OF THE LOCK AND GUN, ALPHABETICALLY ARRANGED.

Antechamber. — The small opening or passage forming a connection between the end of the tube and the chamber, and through which the fire from the cap is conducted to the powder lying in the chamber.

Bolts. — The small sliding pin that passes through the fore-end of the stock, and, fitting in the loops of the barrel, secures them in their position.

Bolt-Loops. — Small iron loops, attached to the barrels, through which the bolts pass to fasten the barrel to the stock.

Break-off or *False Breeching.* — The piece of metal made fast to the stock by the cross-pin, into which the hooks of the breeches must be inserted before the barrels will slip into their bed.

Bridle. — The piece of polished steel, partly covering the tumbler and scear in which the pivot of the tumbler works, holding all the machinery secure.

Bridle-Pins. — Small screws which keep the bridle in its place.

Cap. — The piece of metal covering the worm of the ramrod.

Cap. — The metal finish at the extreme point of the stock.

Chain or *Swivel*. — A small piece of steel fastened to the neck of the tumbler to receive the end of the mainspring.

Chamber or *Cup*. — The space or opening in the centre of the breech, designed to hold a portion of the charge of powder.

Cock, *Hammer*, or *Striker*. — The arm of the lock, which, being freed by the pressure of the finger on the trigger, falls on the nipple, and explodes the cap.

Cross-Pin or *False-Breech Screw*. — The screw which, passing through the trigger-plate and stock, secures the break-off, or false breeching.

Cup. — See *Chamber*.

Escutcheons. — Pieces of metal set in the stock through which the bolts pass, so as to prevent the wearing or chafing of the wood work. Also the metal shield or thumbpiece on which the crest or name is engraved.

Face or *Head of the Hammer*. — That portion of the cock surrounded with a rim, guard, or nose, which, on its fall, comes in contact with the nipple and explodes the cap.

False Breeching. — See *Break-off*.

False-Breech Screw. — See *Cross-Pin*.

Guard. — Curved plate of metal to protect the trigger.

Guard-Screws. — The screws by which the guard is fastened to the stock.

Hammer. — See *Cock*.

Hammer Bridle. — That portion of the lock in which the tail of the hammer works.

Hammer-Spring. — The pin on which the tail of the hammer is moved.

Head of the Hammer. — See *Face of the Hammer*.

Heel-Plate. — The plate with which the butt is tipped.

Heel-Plate Screws. — Screws which secure the heel-plate to the stock.

Lock-Plate. — Plate to which the works of the lock are attached.

Main-Spring. — The large spring attached to the swivel by which the lock is worked.

Nipple, Pivot, or *Tube.* — The small steel pillar screwed into the breeches, on which the copper cap is placed.

Patent Breech. — The piece of metal which is screwed into the end of the barrel and forms the chamber.

Pipes. — Bands to receive the ramrod.

Pivot. — See *Nipple.*

Ramrod-Head. — The piece of metal which, surrounding the head of the ramrod, prevents it from splitting.

Ramrod-Screw or *Worm.* — The screw at the end of the rod for the purpose of drawing a wad.

Rod-Stop. — The small piece of metal on the inner side of the barrel, contiguous to the muzzle, which prevents the ramrod from slipping out.

Scear. — The small piece of metal which catches in the bends of the tumblers for whole or half-cock, and, when pushed out of position by the trigger, permits the cock to fall on the cap.

Screw-Pin. — The small screw which passes through the scear into the lock-plate, and keeps it in its proper position.

Scear-Spring. — The spring which forces and holds the scear in the bends or notches of the tumbler.

Scear-Spring Screw. — The screw which keeps the scear-spring in its place.

Scroll-Guard. — Extension of the guard to protect the hand.

Side-Pin or *Nail.* — The screw which holds the lock to the stock.

Sight. — The piece of metal attached to the rib which connects the barrels, put on the top, and near the muzzle, used in taking aim at any object.

Sight-Plate. — See *Top-Piece.*

Spring-Cramp. — An instrument for taking out the mainspring.

Stock. — The wooden part of the gun, which supports the barrel, and comes to the shoulder in shooting.

Striker. — See *Cock.*

Swivel. — See *Chain.*

Top-Piece, *Sight-Plate*, or *Upper-Rib.* — The elevated metal plate along which the eye is directed to the sight.

Triggers. — Light pieces of metal, protected by the guard, and extending to the interior of the lock, which, upon being pressed by the finger, withdraw the scear from the tumbler, and thus permit the cock to fall and explode the cap.

Trigger-Plate. — The plate in which the trigger works.

Trigger-Spring. — The small spring that, pressing against the trigger, keeps it close to the scear.

Tube. — See *Nipple.*

Tumbler. — The movable centre-piece of a lock, having an axle passing through the lock-plate to which the cock is fastened.

Tumbler-Screw or *Pin.* — The screw with which the cock or hammer is fastened to the tumbler.

Under-Cross Pin. — The screw which passes through the front of the guard or trigger-plate into the base of the break-off.

Under-Rib. — The piece of metal running the whole length of the barrels, which, together with the upper rib or sight-plate, holds them securely together.

Vent or *Vent-Hole.* — A small hole at the side of the breeching, intended to allow the escape of a portion of the explosive force, and lessen the recoil.

TERMS USED BY SPORTSMEN.

For Woodcock.

A couple of Woodcocks.
A couple and a half of Woodcocks.
A flight of Woodcocks.
To flush or start Woodcocks.

For Partridges or Quails.

A brace of Partridges or birds.
A covey of Partridges or birds.
A brace and a half of Partridges or birds.
To spring or flush Partridges or birds.

For Grouse.

A brood of Grouse.
A pack of Grouse.
A brace of Grouse.
A leash of Grouse.

For Snipe or Plover.

A wisp or walk of Snipes.
A wing or congregation of Plovers.
A couple of Snipes or Plovers.
A couple and a half of Snipes or Plovers.
To spring a Snipe or Plover.

For Large Wild-Fowl.

A flock or team of Wild Ducks.
A company or trip of Wild Ducks.
A gaggle or flock of Wild Geese.
A flock of Teal.
A gang of Brant.
A whiteness of Swans.

For Small Wild-Fowl or Shore Birds of all Kinds.
A flock.
A couple.
A couple and a half.

For Hares.
A brace of Hares.
A leash of Hares.
To start a Hare.

CONSTITUTION AND BY-LAWS OF THE WINTHROP SHOOTING-CLUB OF BOSTON,

WITH THE RULES OF TRAP-SHOOTING.

CONSTITUTION.

NAME.

ARTICLE 1. This Club shall be called the "——— Club."

OFFICERS.

ART. 2. The officers shall consist of a President, Secretary, and Treasurer. There shall also be an Executive Committee, consisting of five persons, three of whom shall be the officers above named. They shall all be chosen with ballot by general ticket, and shall hold their offices for one year, or until others shall be chosen in their stead. A majority of all the votes cast at a legal meeting of the Club shall be required for an election. An election of officers shall take place immediately after the adoption of the Constitution and By-Laws, for the period extending to the first annual election, on the second Thursday in ———, 186-.

DUTIES OF THE PRESIDENT.

ART. 3. It shall be the duty of the President, when present, to preside at all meetings of the Club and Executive Committee ; to preserve order ; see that the laws of the Club are promptly executed, and the rules of parliamentary usage are observed in respect to precedence of motions, orders of debate, &c. ; but if he wishes to take the floor to discuss any motion, he must call some one to preside. In case of an equal division of the members on any question, the presiding officer shall give the casting vote. He shall call special meetings of the Club when he shall deem it expedient, or the interests of the Club require it ; and on the written application of five members shall call a meeting at such time as they shall designate. He shall issue notices of meetings, in case of the absence or incapacity of the Secretary.

DUTIES OF THE SECRETARY.

ART. 4. It shall be the duty of the Secretary, in case of the absence of the President, to call the meetings to order, when a President *pro tem.* shall be elected. He shall keep a record of the proceedings of the meetings of the Club and Executive Committee, with such record of the shoots as the Executive Committee or Club may deem expedient; shall issue all notices of meetings, stating therein the time and place of said meeting, and the business coming before it ; shall collect all assessments, and pay the same into the treasury ; and any notice sent to a member, through the post-office, of assessments due, shall be considered as a demand for the same. He shall also keep a record of the name in full of each member of the Club, his residence and business ; which records, books, and papers shall be open to the inspection of the members at all reasonable times. At the end of his term of office, he shall deliver all the books, papers, and records of the Club in good order into the hands of his successor.

DUTIES OF THE TREASURER.

ART. 5. It shall be the duty of the Treasurer to keep open to the inspection of the members, at all reasonable times, an accurate account of all money received into the treasury from the Secretary or otherwise, and of all the expenditures of the Club, and make a report in writing of the same, at the annual meeting on the ——— of each year. Said report must have been audited and approved by the Executive Committee, and must be received and acted upon previous to the election of officers. He shall pay all bills of accounts approved by the Executive Committee ; and, at the end of his term of office, shall surrender all books, papers, and moneys of the Club, in his hands, into the hands of his successor.

DUTIES OF THE EXECUTIVE COMMITTEE.

ART. 6. The Executive Committee shall have power to make such rules and regulations as may be found necessary for the better management of the Club, which shall be submitted to the members for their approval, at their next legal meeting. They shall have charge of, and be responsible for, all the property of the Club ; shall make arrangements for all shoots, designating time and place ; purchase pigeons, provide collation, and grounds to shoot upon, and appoint judges or referees to decide any dispute that may arise upon the same ; but said judges or referees shall confine themselves to the By-Laws of the Club. They may hold meetings for business as often as they deem the interests of the Club require. They shall audit, and, if found correct, approve the books and accounts of the Treasurer, and also approve all bills of accounts against the Club, which bills so approved shall be equivalent to a draft on the treasury for the same. On a petition of five members, the Executive Committee shall appoint a day for a shoot; but at all shoots, the party shooting shall pay all expenses attending the same, — such as cost of pigeons and keeping the same, lunch, &c., excepting on an annual shoot, when each member of the Club shall be assessed his proportion of expenses, whether he be present or no.

MEMBERS.

ART. 7. The number of members of the Club shall be unlimited. Should the number be decreased by death or otherwise, new members may be elected in their stead, by a two-thirds vote of all members present at any legal meeting of the Club; such new member to have been proposed at a previous meeting; and the notice for the call of the meeting shall so specify. Each member shall pay into the treasury on entering the Club five dollars; and an annual assessment of two dollars at the commencement of each year thereafter; and any member neglecting or refusing to pay any assessment for thirty days from demand shall forfeit to the Club all his rights to any property of the same; also all rights to membership, unless such delinquent shall make a reasonable excuse at the next legal meeting, which excuse shall be accepted by a two-thirds vote of said meeting. Each member shall notify the Secretary of any change of residence or business. Any member being noisy, disorderly, disrespectful, or offensive, may be *expelled*, by a two-thirds vote, at any legal meeting, and their property in the Club confiscated to the use of the same. Every member shall sign this Constitution.

QUORUM.

ART. 8, SEC. 1. At any meeting of the Club, nine members shall constitute a quorum for business.

Sec. 2. At any meeting of the Executive Committee, three members shall constitute a quorum.

MEETINGS.

Art. 9. There shall be held a meeting of the Club on ―――― in each year, to receive and act upon the report of the Treasurer and Executive Committee, and any other business that may then come before them; after which an election of officers shall take place. Should a vacancy occur in any office, a meeting shall at once be called to fill such vacancy. No meeting to be legal, except notice be given, at least three days previous to said meeting.

AMENDMENTS.

Art. 10. No alteration or amendment of this Constitution shall be made, except by a vote of a majority of all the members of the Club, at a meeting called for that purpose, notice of which shall be given at least five days previous to said meeting; and said notice shall expressly specify that said meeting is for the purpose of amending or altering the Constitution. The By-Laws may be altered or amended by a majority of the members present at any legal meeting; notice of which alteration or amendment shall have been given at a previous meeting, and so specified in the call for said meeting.

BY-LAWS.

Article 1. If the officers of this Club, in their several official capacities, shall neglect the performance of their duties, or shall not administer the laws of the Club efficiently and equally, on written complaint of five members a meeting shall be called, at which meeting the accused may be censured, removed from office, or fully exonerated, as the circumstances of the case may warrant.

ORDER OF PROCEEDINGS.

ART. 2, SEC. 1. Secretary to first read record of the last meeting, which, being approved, shall stand. When a motion has been made and seconded, it shall be put in writing if desired by any member, and read by the Chairman before the same be open for discussion.

SEC. 2. When a motion is under discussion, all remarks must be addressed to the Chair; and no other motion shall be entertained, except to amend, adjourn, lay on the table, postpone indefinitely, or call for the previous question, which several motions shall have precedence in the order in which they stand arranged.

SEC. 3. No member who did not vote with the majority on any question shall move the reconsideration of a vote.

SEC. 4. Voting by proxy shall not be allowed in this Club.

ART. 3. The Executive Committee shall report in writing at each annual meeting of the Club, of their doings, of the amount and character of the property of the Club in their charge; which report shall be placed on file, and kept by the Secretary for the use of members.

ART. 4. No assessments shall be laid on the members of the Club, other than such as are provided for by the Constitution, except by the votes of two thirds of all the members present at any legal meeting.

Any member wishing to withdraw from the Club must notify the Secretary of such intention.

ART. 5. The Executive Committee may invite one or more distinguished shots to participate in any shoot; such invited guest to be subject to the rules, and pay the same as a member of the Club. All guns to be discharged immediately upon the close of any shoot.

No liquor shall be furnished by the Club or Executive

Committee to be drank upon the ground or elsewhere. No money to be drawn from the treasury to pay for pigeons.

In cases of a match or sweepstakes, the Club to be governed by the rules of the New York Club, hereunto appended.

Signed, ———, *President*.
———, *Secretary*.
———, *Treasurer*.

RULES OF TRAP-SHOOTING ADOPTED BY THE NEW YORK SPORTSMEN'S CLUB.

JUDGES.

1st. All matches or sweepstakes to be under the direction of two judges, to be appointed by the parties interested from members of the Club ; and in the event of any difference of opinion between them, they are to choose a referee, whose decision shall be final.

TRAPS.

2d. Ground-traps are to be used, unless otherwise agreed upon by the parties interested.

3d. In shooting with two traps, the choice of either must be decided by lot.

4th. In double-bird shooting, two traps must be used, unless otherwise agreed upon, placed six feet apart, and the lines so attached that both traps may be pulled together.

GUNS.

5th. The use of single or double barrelled guns to be specified at the time of making a match, or entering a sweepstakes.

SHOT.

6th. The *weight of shot* not to exceed one and a half ounces either for single or double birds.

APPENDIX. 263

7th. Any person or persons using a greater weight of shot than this, unless an increase of it shall have been specified or agreed upon, loses his claim in the result of the match, or sweepstakes, as the case may be.

RISE.

8th. The *rise* for single birds to be twenty-one yards, and for double birds eighteen yards.

BOUNDARIES.

9th. The *boundary* for single birds to be eighty yards and for double birds one hundred yards; the distances being measured from the trap.

10th. If a bird is once out of bounds, it is missed.

SCORING.

11th. When a person is at the *score*, and ready to shoot, he is to call *pull:* and should the trap be sprung without his having given the word, he may take the bird or birds or not; but if he shoots, the bird or birds will be charged to him.

12th. The party at the score must not leave it to shoot.

13th. The party shooting is to be at the score within the expiration of five minutes from the last shot; but in the event of any delay beyond his control, he may claim fifteen minutes once in the course of a match or sweepstakes.

14th. When a party is at the score, no one will be permitted to go in front of him to put a bird up, in the event of its not rising readily.

15th. The party at the score must hold the but of his gun below his elbow, until the bird or birds rise.

RISING OF BIRDS.

16th. If the trap or traps are sprung, and the bird or birds do not rise in a reasonable time, either of the judges may declare "no bird"; but if they do not say "no bird," the party at the score must wait for the bird or birds to rise.

17th. In double-bird shooting, should only one bird fly, it is to be charged to the party shooting, whether he may have shot or not.

18th. Should two birds be killed with one barrel, they are to be credited to the party shooting.

19th. If a bird or birds walk away from the trap, the judges may declare "no bird."

20th. A bird must be on the wing when shot at.

MISSING FIRE.

21st. In case a percussion-cap or primer, as the case may be, fails to explode, the bird or birds are not to be charged to the party shooting; but if the cap or primer explodes without igniting a charge, or if, after his giving the word to pull, his gun proves not to have been cocked, or not to have been properly loaded, and it fails to fire, he will be held to have missed.

BALKING.

22d. If, in the opinion of the judges, the party at the score is balked, or in any manner obstructed by his opponent, or any person other than his own backers, he may be allowed to trap another bird, in accordance with the decision of the judges.

23d. In single-bird shooting, when more than one rises at a time, either of the judges may call "no bird," if he or they think proper; but if the party at the score has shot at a bird, it will be charged to him.

24th. If a bird or birds shall fly towards the parties within the bounds, in such a manner that to shoot at them would involve the wounding of any of the parties referred to, the judges, or either of them, may decide "no bird."

25th. If a bird in its flight is shot at by another party

than the one at the score, and is recovered within the bounds, the judges are to decide if the bird was missed by the party at the score.

26th. If at any time it should so occur that different and opposing orders should be given by the judges to a party at the score, he is to arrest his fire ; and any bird shot at by him after such orders shall not be allowed him if recovered, or charged to him if missed.

TIES.

27th. In case of a *tie*, it must be shot off the same day, if practicable to do so, unless the purse, or prizes, are divided by agreement ; and if not, it must be decided the *first* ensuing fitting day.

28th. In the decision of ties, three shots will be required both for double and single birds, except otherwise agreed upon.

RECOVERING OF BIRDS.

29th. The party shooting must gather his birds individually, if required to do so by his opponent.

30th. The party recovering a bird must use his hands alone.

31st. If a bird alights in a tree, or upon any place impracticable to be conveniently recovered, the party shooting will be allowed fifteen minutes for the bird to fall or change his resting-place ; if he is not recovered in that time, it will be held to be a missed bird.

SECTIONS OF THE GAME-LAWS OF THE STATE OF MASSACHUSETTS ENACTED FOR THE PROTECTION OF CERTAIN BIRDS AND ANIMALS.

SECTION 1. Whoever, between the first day of March and the first day of October, takes, kills, or destroys any of the birds called partridges or quails ; or between the first day of March and the fourth day of July, takes, kills, or destroys any of, the birds called woodcock ; or at any season of the year takes, kills, or destroys any of the birds called robins, thrushes, linnets, sparrows, bluebirds, bobolinks, yellowbirds, woodpeckers, or warblers, or within the respective times aforesaid sells, buys, or has in his possession any of said birds taken or killed in this State or elsewhere, shall forfeit for every such partridge, quail, or woodcock, five dollars, and for every other of said birds two dollars.

SEC. 2. Whoever, at any season of the year, takes, kills, or destroys, by means of traps or snares, any of the birds mentioned in the preceding section, except partridges, shall forfeit for every such bird so taken, killed, or destroyed, five dollars.

SEC. 3. The mayor and aldermen and selectmen of the several cities and towns shall cause the provisions of the preceding sections to be enforced in their respective places.

SEC. 4. Whoever, between the first day of March and the fourth day of July, shoots at or kills any birds upon lands not owned or occupied by himself, and without license from the owner or occupant thereof, shall forfeit to the owner or occupant ten dollars, in addition to the actual damages sustained, to be recovered in an action of tort.

SEC. 5. Whoever, between the first day of March and the first day of July, takes or kills any birds on any saltmarshes, or sells any birds so taken or killed, shall forfeit two dollars for every offence ; provided, that nothing contained in this section shall prevent the owner or occupant of such lands from taking or killing birds on lands so owned or held by him.

SEC. 6. Whoever, within this State, takes, kills, or destroys any of the birds called grouse or heath-hens, or sells, buys, or has in his possession any of said birds so killed or taken, shall forfeit for every such bird twenty dollars.

SEC. 7. Whoever kills any grouse or heath-hen as aforesaid, upon lands not owned or occupied by himself, and without license from the owner or occupant thereof, shall, for each bird so killed, forfeit to such owner or occupant ten dollars, in addition to the actual damages sustained, to be recovered in an action of tort.

SEC. 8. When a person is suspected of having in his possession grouse or heath-hen taken or killed contrary to the provision of this chapter, a justice of the peace or police court, on complaint, on oath before him, may issue his warrant directed to the proper officer, to search for the same; and the same proceedings may be had as are provided in chapter one hundred and seventy, relating to searches and seizures.

SEC. 9. The provisions of the preceding sections shall not extend to any city in which the city council, nor to any town in which the inhabitants at their annual meeting, in any year, vote to suspend the operation thereof in whole or in part, and for such term of time, not exceeding one year, as they deem expedient.

SEC. 10. Whoever, between the hour of sunset and one hour before the sun's rising, on any day between the twentieth day of April and the first day of July, takes, confines, kills, or destroys any of the birds called plover, curlin, doughbird, or chicken-bird, shall, for every such bird so taken, confined, killed, or destroyed, forfeit one dollar.

SEC. 11. Whoever at any time kills or destroys any of the birds mentioned in the preceding section, by the use of any other means or instruments than such as are usually used in fowling or killing wild game, shall, for every such offence, be liable to the penalty mentioned in said section.

SEC. 12. Whoever, between the first day of January and

the first day of August, kills or hunts any deer, except his own tame deer, or deer kept in his park or on his own land, shall, for every such offence, forfeit twenty dollars.

Sec. 13. Whoever, at any time of the year, hunts, chases, or kills, with hounds or dogs, any deer within the counties of Plymouth or Barnstable, shall, for every such offence, forfeit twenty dollars.

SECTIONS OF THE GAME-LAWS OF THE STATE OF NEW YORK APPLICABLE TO THE HUNTING OF DEER, WILD FOWL, AND BIRDS.

MOOSE AND DEER.

Section 1. No person shall kill, or pursue with intent to kill, any moose or wild deer, save only during the months of August, September, October, November, and up to and inclusive of the tenth day of December, or shall expose for sale, or have in his or her possession, any green moose or deer skin, or fresh venison, save only in the months aforesaid, and up to and inclusive of the tenth of December.

WILD FAWN AND GRAY RABBITS.

Sec. 2. No person shall at any time kill any wild fawn during the periods when such fawn is in its spotted coat, or expose for sale, or have at any time in his or her possession any spotted wild fawn skin or any gray rabbit from the first of February to the first of November.

WILD PIGEONS.

Sec. 3. No person shall kill or catch, or discharge any fire-arm at, any wild pigeon while in any nesting ground, or break up or in any manner disturb such nesting ground or the nests or birds therein, or discharge any fire-arm at any distance within one fourth mile of such nesting place at such pigeon.

WILD FOWL.

SEC. 4. No person shall kill or expose for sale, or have in his possession after the same is killed, any wood duck (commonly called black duck), gray duck (commonly called summer duck), mallard or teal duck, between the first day of February and the fifteenth day of August in each year. No person shall at any time kill any wild duck, goose, or other wild fowl, with or by means of the device or instrument known as swivel or punt gun, or with or by means of any gun other than such guns as are habitually raised at arm's length, and fired from the shoulder, or shall use any such device, or instrument or gun, other than such gun as aforesaid, with intent to kill any such duck, goose, or other wild fowl. No person shall in any manner kill, or molest with intent to kill, any wild ducks, geese, or other wild fowl, while the same are sitting at night upon their resting-places. But this section shall not apply to waters of Long Island Sound or the Atlantic Ocean.

PENALTY FOR VIOLATION.

SEC. 5. Any person violating the foregoing provisions of this act shall be deemed guilty of a misdemeanor, and shall likewise be liable to a penalty of fifty dollars for each offence.

INSECTIVOROUS BIRDS.

SEC. 6. No person shall at any time, within this State, kill or trap, or expose for sale, or have in his possession, after the same is killed, any eagle, fish-hawk, night-hawk, whippoorwill, finch, thrush, lark, sparrow, yellow-bird, brown thresher, wren, martin, swallow, tanager, oriole, woodpecker, bobolink, or any other harmless bird, or any song-bird ; or kill, trap or expose for sale any robin, blackbird, meadow lark or starling, save during the months of August, September, October, November, and December; nor destroy or rob the nests of any wild birds whatever, under a penalty of five dollars for each bird so killed, trapped, or exposed for sale, and for each nest destroyed or robbed. This section shall not apply to any person who shall kill or trap any bird for the purpose of studying its habits or history, or having the same stuffed and set up as a specimen; nor to any person who shall kill on his own premises any robin during the period when summer fruits or grapes are ripening, provided such robin is killed in the act of destroying such fruits or grapes.

PINNATED GROUSE.

SEC. 7. No person shall, at any time within ten years from the passage of this act, kill any pinnated grouse, commonly called the prairie fowl, unless upon grounds owned by them, and grouse placed thereon by said owners, under a penalty of ten dollars for each bird so killed.

WOODCOCK, RUFFED GROUSE, QUAIL, RAIL, AND PARTRIDGE.

SEC. 8. No person shall kill, or have in his or her possession, except alive, for the purpose of preserving the same alive through the winter, or expose for sale any woodcock or ruffed grouse, commonly called partridge, between the first day of January and the first day of September, or kill any quail, sometimes called Virginia partridge, between the first day of January and the twentieth day of October, or have the same in possession, or expose the same for sale between the first day of February and the twentieth day of October, or have in his possession any pinnated grouse, commonly called prairie chicken, or expose the same for sale between the first day of February and the first day of July, under a penalty of five dollars for each bird so killed or had in possession, or exposed for sale. Provided, however, that in the counties lying along the Hudson River and Susquehanna River and its branches, and in the counties lying south of the north line of the county of Greene and the county of Columbia, and in the counties bordering upon the waters where the tide ebbs and flows, it shall be lawful to kill or possess or expose for sale any woodcock or rail or ruffed grouse, commonly called partridge, between the third day of July and the first day of January.

TRAPPING PROHIBITED.

SEC. 9. No person shall, at any time, or in any place within this State, with any trap or snare, take any quail or ruffed grouse, under a penalty of five dollars for each quail or grouse so trapped or snared.

VIOLATING THE SABBATH.

SEC. 10. There shall be no shooting, hunting, or trapping on the first day of the week, called Sunday, and any person offending against the provisions of this section shall, on conviction, forfeit and pay a sum not exceeding twenty-five dollars, or be imprisoned in the county jail of the county where the offence was committed, not less than ten days nor more than twenty-five days for each offence.

TRESPASS.

SEC. 11. Any person who shall at any time enter upon the lawn, garden, orchard, or pleasure grounds immediately surrounding a dwelling-house, with any fire-arm, for the purpose of shooting, contrary to the provisions of this act, or shall shoot at any bird or animal thereon, shall be deemed guilty of trespass, and in addition to the damages, shall be liable to a penalty of ten dollars.

APPENDIX.

HOW PENALTIES ARE RECOVERED.

SEC. 20. All penalties imposed under the provisions of this act may be recovered, with cost of suit, by any person or persons in his or their own names, before any justice of the peace in the county where the offence was committed or where the defendant resides ; or when such suit shall be brought in the city of New York, before any justice of any of the District Courts or of the Marine Court of said city ; or such penalties may be recovered in an action in the Supreme Court of this State, by any person or persons, in his or their own names ; which action shall be governed by the same rules as other actions in said Supreme Court, except that a recovery by the plaintiff or plaintiffs in such suit in said court, costs shall be allowed to such plaintiff or plaintiffs, without regard to the amount of such recovery ; and any district court judge, justice of the peace, police, or other magistrate, is authorized, upon receiving sufficient security for costs on the part of the complainant, and sufficient proof by affidavit of the violation of the provisions of this act, by any person being temporarily within his jurisdiction but not residing therein, or by any person whose name and residence are unknown, to issue his warrant and have such offender committed or held to bail to answer the charge against him ; and any district court judge, justice of the peace, police, or other magistrate may, upon proof of probable cause to believe in the concealment of any game or fish mentioned in this act, during any of the prohibited periods, issue his search-warrant and cause search to be made in any house, market-boat, car, or other building, and for that end may cause any apartment, chest, box, locker, or crate to be broken open and the contents examined. Any penalties, when collected, shall be paid by the court before which conviction shall be had, one half to the overseers of the poor, for the use of the poor of the town in which conviction is had, and the remainder to the prosecutor. On the nonpayment of the penalty, the defendant shall be committed to the common jail of the county for a period of not less than five days, and at the rate of one day for each dollar of the amount of the judgment, where the sum is over five dollars in amount. Any court of special sessions in this State shall have jurisdiction to try and dispose of all and any of the offences arising in the same county against the provisions of this act ; and every justice of the peace shall have jurisdiction within his county of actions to recover any penalty hereby given or created.

POSSESSION OF GAME PRIOR TO PROHIBITED PERIOD.

SEC. 21. Any person proving that the birds, fish, skins, or animals found in his or her possession during the prohibited periods, were killed prior to such periods, or were killed in any place outside of the limits of this State, and that the law of such place did not prohibit such killing, shall be exempted from the penalties of this act.

COMMON CARRIERS AND EXPRESS COMPANIES.

SEC. 22. In all prosecutions under this act, it shall be competent for common carriers or express companies to show that the inhibited article in his or their possession came into such possession in another State, in which State the law did not prohibit such possession, and such showing shall be deemed a defence in such prosecution. No action for a penalty under the provisions of this act shall be settled or compromised, except upon the payment into court of the full amount of such penalty, unless upon such terms and conditions as may be imposed by the district attorney of the county in which such action shall have been brought.

SUMMARY.

THE following summary of the game-laws, with reference to the killing of woodcock, partridges, quails, and deer in the States named, is copied from the statute-books of the respective States. The killing of the above-mentioned game is prohibited as follows: —

	Woodcock.	Partridges.	Quails.	Deer.
Maine	Not at all.	Not at all.	Not at all.	Between Jan. 15 and Sept. 1.
New Hampshire	Between Feb. 1 and July 1.	Between Feb. 1 and Sept. 1.	Between Feb. 1 and Sept. 1.	Between Feb. 1 and Aug. 1.
Vermont	Not at all.	Not at all.	Not at all.	Between Jan. 10 and July 1.
Massachusetts	Between Mar. 1 and Sept. 15.	Between Mar. 1 and Sept. 1.	Between Jan. 1 and Sept. 1.	Between Jan. 1 and Aug. 1.
Rhode Island	Between Jan. 1 and July 4.	Between Jan. 1 and Sept. 20.	Between Feb. 1 and Oct. 1.	
Connecticut	Between Feb. 1 and July 4.	Between Feb. 1 and Sept. 1.	Between Feb. 1 and Oct. 1.	
New York	Between Jan. 1 and Sept. 1.	Between Jan. 1 and Sept. 1.	Between Jan. 1 and Oct. 20.	Between Dec. 10 & July 31.
New Jersey	Between Jan. 1 and July 4.	Between Jan. 1 and Nov. 1.	Between Jan. 1 and Sept. 1.	Between Jan. 2 and Aug. 31.
Illinois	Between Jan. 1 and July 1.	Between Jan. 1 and Aug. 15.	Between Jan. 1 and Aug. 15.	Between Jan. 1 and Aug. 15.
Indiana	Not at all.	Between Feb. 1 and Oct. 1.	Between Feb. 1 and Oct. 1.	Between Jan. 1 and Oct. 1
Michigan	Between Mar 1 and July 1.	Between Feb. 1 and Sept. 1.	Between Jan. 1 and Oct. 1.	Between Jan. 15 and Sept. 1.
Iowa	Between Jan. 1 and July 1.	Between Dec. 15 & Sept. 12.	Between Dec. 15 & Sept. 12.	Between Jan. 1 and Aug. 1.
Ohio	Between Feb. 1 and July 4	Between Feb. 1 and Oct. 15.	Between Feb. 1 and Oct. 15.	
Wisconsin	Between Dec. 1 and July 4.	Between Dec. 15 & Aug. 20.	Between Dec. 15 & Aug. 20.	Between Jan. 15 and Aug. 1.

THE END.

Cambridge: Electrotyped and Printed by Welch, Bigelow, & Co.

ALLEN'S
NEW PATENT BREECH-LOADING
DOUBLE-BARREL SHOT GUN,

MANUFACTURED BY

ETHAN ALLEN & CO.,
Worcester, Mass.

The cut below represents the gun with the lid open, the guard down, and a cartridge partly withdrawn. Also a longitudinal section of a loaded cartridge shell, showing the conical, or patent chamber form, which is acknowledged to be one of the most desirable features in all good guns.

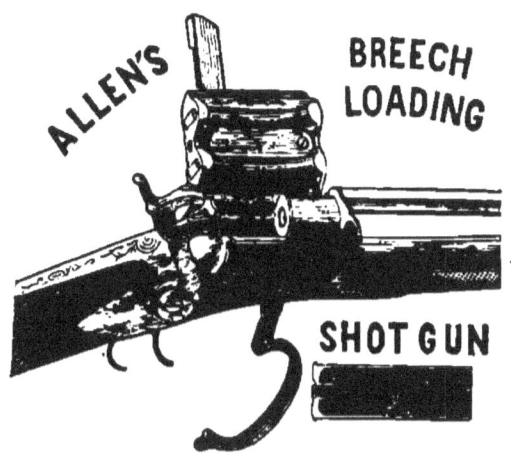

These guns are remarkably strong shooters, and use steel cartridge cases, which will last as long as the gun, and the cartridges can be inserted in the barrels quicker than in any other breech-loader made.

PRICE LIST.

For **Fine Stub Twist**, oiled or varnished Stock, well engraved, $100
For **Fine Laminated and Damascus**, oiled or varnished Stock, finely engraved $150
☞ *A Cartridge Case, 24 Steel Shells, Loader and Brush, are furnished with each Gun.*
Extra Shells . . . . $6.00 per dozen.
Primers . . . . $2.50 per M.

We also manufacture

MUZZLE-LOADING DOUBLE-BARREL SHOT GUNS

of all grades, from $35 upwards, and warranted superior to foreign-made guns of the same price.

JOHN P. LOVELL & SONS, Agents,
27 Dock Square and 15 Washington Street, BOSTON.

THE HAZARD POWDER CO.

Manufacturers and Dealers in

Sporting, Rifle, and Target

GUNPOWDER,

Continue to furnish these well-known brands:

"**Electric**" **Gunpowder,** in 1 lb. canisters.

"**American Sporting,**" in 1 lb. canisters and $6\frac{1}{4}$ lb. kegs.

"**Duck Shooting,**" in 1 lb. and 5 lb. canisters, and in kegs of $12\frac{1}{2}$ and $6\frac{1}{4}$ lbs. each.

"**Kentucky Rifle,**" in 1 lb. and 5 lb. canisters,

"**Kentucky Rifle,**" in 25, $12\frac{1}{2}$, $6\frac{1}{4}$ lb. kegs.

"**Deer Powder,**" in kegs and canisters.

CANNON AND MUSKET POWDER.

Shipping, Mining, and Blasting Powder.

The above well-known GUNPOWDERS are supplied by the Company's Agents in every prominent city, and in the various mining districts of the United States, and by all dealers in Guns and Sporting materials, or wholesale at the office of the Company,

89 WALL STREET, NEW YORK.

THOS. S. POPE, SEC'Y. A. G. HAZARD, PRES.

"JOSEPH TONKS,"

MANUFACTURER OF

Superior Single and Double Barrelled

SHOT GUNS,

AT No. 49 UNION STREET,

Corner of Marshall Street, . . . BOSTON.

Mr. Tonks received the

GOLD MEDAL FOR SUPERIOR WORKMANSHIP

AT THE

10th EXHIBITION OF MASSACHUSETTS MECHANICS' ASSOCIATION, HELD AT BOSTON, SEPTEMBER, 1865.

Mr. Tonks manufactures

Double-Barrelled Breech-Loading Shot Guns,

OF THE "LEFAUCHEAUX" AND "CENTRAL FIRE" PLANS, and he adapts the latter to the use of

PAPER, BRASS, OR STEEL CARTRIDGE CASES,

as desired.

Mr. Tonks also re-bores any Shot Gun that is of sufficient thickness, and makes it shoot as desired.

Mr. Tonks keeps constantly on hand a variety of ready-made

SHOT GUNS AND AIR GUNS,

with a full complement of

All kinds of Sporting Apparatus, and is a Repairer of all kinds of Fire-Arms.

ORANGE SPORTING POWDER.

THE PRIZE POWDER OF THE WORLD.

This Powder has greater strength and range, and leaves less residuum, than any other, and that of an oily nature, so that *comparatively there is no fouling*. In the experiments made by the Russian Officers (the most exhaustive of any ever made, and running through a period of fifteen months), there were fired *ten thousand rounds of this powder* from two rifles, and without once washing the rifles, and without once missing fire, a feat never paralleled in the annals of gunnery. After testing all the principal brands, they gave their orders for Orange Powder, and adopted *this* as their standard hereafter.

Before the Examining Board in Washington, August, 1866, it proved superior to all others.

At the Wimbleton Rifle Meeting in England, July, 1866, in competition with the best foreign powders, *it won the first prize*.

The Board convened by the Commander-in-Chief of the State of New York, for the examination of military small arms, whose sessions were attended by officers specially detached by the Russian, Prussian, and Danish Governments, say, in their printed report of the numerous guns on trial, that after firing 100 rounds, all but one became so foul as not to admit the cartridge.

This led to a test of the *powder*, and they deem this subject of so much importance that they say in their report: "The *powder used in these cartridges, which did not foul the gun, deserves special mention* as being *very superior.* It is the Orange Rifle Powder."

In their Supplementary Report, March 27th, 1868, they say: "The results of the recent trials induce no modification of the favorable opinion of this powder as previously expressed."

After firing one hundred rounds of seventy grains each, the residuum left in the barrel weighed less than a grain, while the United States Musket Powder fouled the barrel excessively.

In shooting-matches it has been universally successful. The celebrated trap shooters, John and William Taylor, of Jersey City, say: "It is the best powder we have ever used."

One of the best sportsmen in this State writes: "With the Orange Powder I made the largest score I ever made." Another celebrated shot, from Central New York, writes: "Your powder is in high repute here, and the country round about, and will supersede all others,"—and this is the tone of all the best sportsmen who have tested it.

OUR PRINCIPAL BRANDS ARE:

ORANGE LIGHTNING,

ORANGE DUCKING,

ORANGE GAME,

ORANGE RIFLE.

MANUFACTURED BY

SMITH & RAND POWDER CO.,

No. 170 BROADWAY, NEW YORK,

And for sale by Dealers generally.

JOHN P. LOVELL & SONS,

IMPORTERS AND DEALERS IN

GUNS, FISHING-TACKLE,

GUN MATERIALS, POWDER-FLASKS,
POCKET CUTLERY, SHOT-POUCHES,
METALLIC CARTRIDGES, CAPS, WADS, &c.

Smith & Wesson, Allen's, Colt's,
AND OTHER
REVOLVERS.

Dog Collars,
GERMAN SILVER, BRASS, AND LEATHER,
In Great Variety.

AGENTS FOR

ETHAN ALLEN & CO.'S BREECH-LOADING
DOUBLE GUNS.

SMITH & RAND'S ORANGE POWDER.
YATHAM'S NEW YORK SHOT.

---

27 Dock Square & 15 Washington Street,
BOSTON.

JOHN P. LOVELL. JOHN W. LOVELL. BENJ. S. LOVELL.

Adventures in the Wilderness;

OR,

CAMP-LIFE IN THE ADIRONDACKS.

BY

REV. WILLIAM H. H. MURRAY.

One volume, nearly 300 pages, beautifully printed from new and clear type, handsomely illustrated with EIGHT FULL-PAGE PICTURES, and bound in morocco cloth. Price, $1.50.

LIST OF CONTENTS.

I. THE WILDERNESS. — WHY I GO THERE, HOW I GET THERE, WHAT I DO THERE, AND WHAT IT COSTS. — II. THE NAMELESS CREEK. (Illustrated.) — III. RUNNING THE RAPIDS. (Illustrated.) — IV. THE BALL. — V. LOON-SHOOTING IN A THUNDER-STORM. (Illustrated.) — VI. CROSSING THE CARRY. (Illustrated.) — VII. ROD AND REEL. (Illustrated.) — VIII. PHANTOM FALLS. (Illustrated.) — IX. JACK-SHOOTING IN A FOGGY NIGHT. (Illustrated.) — X. SABBATH IN THE WOODS. — XI. A RIDE WITH A MAD HORSE IN A FREIGHT-CAR. (Illustrated.)

REV. MR MURRAY, the Pastor of Park Street Church in Boston, presents in this volume a record of his own camp-life experience in the Adirondacks. In the first chapter he points out the best routes to the wilderness, indicates the most desirable hotels, and gives a full list of articles needed, both by ladies and gentlemen, for an outfit. He describes fully the system of "guiding," giving the names of many trustworthy guides. Indeed, he has left nothing in the way of information and advice unsaid; and by the perusal of this chapter any one can be made familiar with all that it is essential to know either for the selection of an outfit, or guidance in those hundred little details of camp-life which, if attempted in ignorance, so often end in failure. This chapter is, in short, a perfect guide-book for sportsmen and tourists in any wild and mountainous region.

The remaining chapters contain descriptions of the writer's experiences on lake and by bivouac. They are ten in number, and range from the light and humorous to the grave and sad. Eight of them are illustrated in the best style of art, from the author's own descriptions.

☞ *Sent by mail to any address on receipt of price by the publishers,*

FIELDS, OSGOOD, & CO.,

124 TREMONT ST., BOSTON, AND 713 BROADWAY, NEW YORK.

www.ingramcontent.com/pod-product-compliance
Lightning Source LLC
Chambersburg PA
CBHW032108230426
43672CB00009B/1668